To Brenda with love

To my children and their spouses

Valerie and Peter

Debbie and Gary

Jonathan and Heidi

To my beautiful grandchildren

Audrey and Noah

Lydia and Henry

Hannah, Jack, and Briana

CONTENTS

PREFACE

Aunt Celia was a remarkable woman. She passed away peacefully in her 98th year. As a child she served as translator and intermediary to the new world when my father's family arrived from the old country with precious little knowledge of English or modernity. All her life she read armfuls of books lugged home from the public library. She boarded a streetcar and two buses each day to attend Los Angeles High School where she could learn Latin, unavailable at her local high school. By the age of 17 she had graduated from normal school and taken her first teaching job in Nevada, too young to be employed by the Los Angeles Unified School District. She contributed hard-earned dollars to help support the family and purchased its first automobile. She was the rudder that guided the ship of immigrants – so able, so strong, yet so fragile and afraid.

Celia spent her life teaching in public schools where few students or administrators recognized her gifts. She never married, never bore children, traveled little, purchased less, and pinched pennies so tightly that she died rich as well as unhappy. How ironic that dear Aunt Celia should be the source of my interest in happiness.

In the early 1960s when I was a graduate student, Celia sent me a copy of Desmond Morris's *The Naked Ape.*[1] I loved the book, and its sequel *The Human Zoo.*[2] Desmond Morris suggested to me

[1] Morris, D. (1967). *The naked ape: A zoologists' study of the human animal.* New York: McGraw-Hill Publishers.

[2] Morris, D. (1969). *The human zoo.* New York: McGraw-Hill Publishers.

that something was wrong with the way we lived and that we may be biologically unsuited to the environments we have created. His thesis was that we are really just hairless primates, better suited to the natural world than to the concrete jungles we call cities. Cities imprison us just as zoos cage their unlucky residents. And we, as they, live unhappily.

A few years later, while teaching Experimental Psychology, I became interested in an emerging field called Environmental Psychology. Consistent with Morris's thesis were scores of studies, on both animals and humans, suggesting that overcrowded cities generate misery and crime. In the 1970s, Environmental Psychology gathered an abundance of evidence that our unhappiness, incivility, and general social pathology was, in one way or another, a consequence of the environments in which we live.[3]

In the early 1980s, a friend, Dr. George Diestel, suggested that I view a series of videos featuring Bill Moyers's interviews of Dr. Mortimer Adler,[4] University of Chicago professor and co-editor of the monumental Great Books of the Western World series. Adler loved Aristotle, as I have come to do, especially the *Nicomachean Ethics* in which Aristotle examines how to achieve a good human life. Adler's discussion of Aristotle's *Ethics* changed the way I viewed the problem of happiness. Morris is partly right; our nature does require a certain range of surroundings but a pastoral setting is not enough to ensure well-being. We are a little closer to the divine than our animal cousins and our needs are quite different.

[3] There are a number of books on environmental and ecological psychology available but two that seem to summarize the field as it was in the 1970s are Altman, I. (1975). *The environment and social behavior: Privacy, personal space, territory, crowding.* Monterey, CA: Brooks/Cole Publishing Co., and Moos, R. H., & Insel, P. M. (Eds.). (1974). *Issues in social ecology: Human milieus.* Palo Alto, CA: National Press Books.

[4] Bill Moyers (1981). *PBS Six Great Ideas: Truth-Goodness-Beauty-Liberty-Equality-Justice.* (The Television Series) with Mortimer Adler. From the Aspen Institute in Colorado.

Our survival and reproduction are essential, but not enough. A good human life requires that we fulfill the potentials inherent in our nature. A bird is meant to fly, an acorn is destined to become an oak tree, a child will become an adult human being. We humans are endowed by nature with a common set of potentials and at the same time, we are uniquely gifted with our very own, individual possibilities. Most of us have the potential to speak, to walk, to be a parent, a friend, or a lover. Adding to our shared human characteristics, each of us is programmed with a unique recipe of other possibilities, some quite strong, others weak and barely noticeable, but all defining our individuality. You may have the potential to be an excellent artist but I was not blessed with that possibility. Our potentials are like the recipe for a complicated dish: a teaspoon of outgoingness, a tablespoon of scientist, half a cup of wife or husband, and a pinch of artist. Now add about a thousand more ingredients in various measures and you have a unique human being, a one and only, a person unlike any other. The possibilities are infinite. Each of us is special, unmatched, and truly one of a kind.

If the world is kind to us our possibilities will blend to form a sound, strong, healthy personality and we will flourish. The artist within us will mature and our potentials for friendship, honesty, and courage will flower as well. If we are able to become ourselves, we will be happy and the world in turn will be a better place. If, however, our musical talents can find no means of expression or our athletic powers go unrecognized and unnurtured, then we will remain frustrated and unfulfilled. None of us will ever know complete fulfillment but the closer we get the better our life will be.

Our potentials can be thought of as needs. If you are lucky enough to be inclined toward athletics, gifted with the desire to help others, or blessed with the ability to draw beautiful pictures, then those inclinations express themselves as needs. Artists need to paint, athletes need to be active, responsible parents need to nurture, and politicians, ideally, need to work at making a better world. Whether the world welcomes our potentials or frustrates them is another story, but we need to note at the outset that both the unique set of potentials within us and the world that accepts or rejects them are at play. Our possibilities are frustrated only at some cost, sometimes at considerable cost. Our uniqueness can be nurtured by the environment in which we develop or it can be discouraged and thwarted but not without damage to the person. Possibilities are needs and needs demand expression. When we are permitted to be ourselves and to satisfy our needs and actualize our potentials, then we live well. Happiness comes from … no, happiness *is* actualizing, becoming our selves, fulfilling our possibilities.

Dear Aunt Celia had so much potential. She was terribly bright, so interested in the world, and so caring. She had so much to give yet was never able to be herself. Her early years were filled with responsibility to family. Like so many children of immigrants she bore the burden of leadership and stability. Given the enormous gap between her abilities and the confining roles that she assumed, her professional life could not have been very fulfilling. Her human relationships were often fragile because of her insecurities and overpowering fear of rejection. Celia's life demonstrates so tragically the importance of fulfillment and its unfortunate opposite. Celia's possibilities were great indeed, but the world in which she lived was less than kind. It failed to recognize her potentials. And she too failed, never really coming to know herself, viewing her potentials as trivial desires to be put aside until the obligations of the day were finished.

Unfortunately, it's too late for Celia but as her life enriched mine, I hope it will touch others. Celia is really the power behind this book. Her gift began my search for an answer to the question of how we should live. Aristotle realized, and I have come to accept his view, that happiness can never be an exact science; no specific instructions will be right for everyone. However, there are general principles that, if correctly applied, can move us all toward a good human life.

1

What Is Happiness?

> We hold these truths to be self-evident, that all men are created equal, that they are endowed by their creator with certain unalienable Rights, that among these are Life, Liberty and the pursuit of Happiness.
>
> Thomas Jefferson, The Declaration of Independence, 1776

I find it astonishing that Thomas Jefferson placed happiness alongside liberty and life itself in the Declaration of Independence. While we don't know for sure why Jefferson included happiness in the document, Darrin McMahon[1] discovered "that formulations linking happiness, life, liberty and property" appeared in a number of colonial constitutions. Thus, interest in happiness seems to have been "in the wind" at the time of America's birth. McMahon also noted that while the delegates to the Continental Congress "scrutinized" every line of Jefferson's draft, "cutting and slashing," not a single one recorded reservations about the "pursuit of happiness." Everyone agrees that happiness is good, but should it be up there with life and liberty, and made so prominent in the founding document of the United States?

Psychologist Jonathan Freedman[2] wrote that when one of his interviewers tried to talk about happiness to people in groups,

[1] McMahon, D. M. (2006). *Happiness: A history.* New York: Atlantic Monthly Press.

[2] Freedman, J. (1978). *Happy people: What happiness is, who has it, and why.* New York: Harcourt Brace Jovanovish.

they joked and gave it no real importance. However, "when she interviewed them alone, the topic became too serious and emotional and people stopped talking." Perhaps Jefferson's idea of happiness is the serious kind, the kind that people have difficulty talking about. In this chapter, we will try to understand Jefferson's view by looking at some of the alternative meanings of happiness.

HAPPINESS AS FEELINGS OF PLEASURE

Most people today think of happiness as a feeling, specifically, a feeling of pleasure. We often link pleasurable events and happiness: "I am happy to meet you." "I'm happy to be home again." "I'm happy with my job." Almost any kind of pleasure seems to make us happy.

Bodily pleasures like food, wine, and sex can certainly be enjoyable, and some scholars still think of them as the keys to happiness.[3] However, it is hard to imagine that Jefferson was thinking of such pleasures when he wrote the Declaration of Independence. If pleasure was really as important as life and liberty, we would probably all be addicted to drugs, sex, and rock and roll. Clearly, we are not. Everybody likes pleasure but most of us wouldn't settle for a life filled with just good feelings. Philosopher Robert Norzick[4] asks us to imagine being hooked to a machine that can stimulate the pleasure centers of the brain on demand so that we could feel good all the time. Most of us would be repulsed by such an arrangement.

It is true, however, that not all pleasures are simple sensory pleasures. Philosopher John Stuart Mill[5] spoke of the "higher pleasures,"

[3] Tannsjo, T. (2007). Narrow hedonism. *Journal of Happiness Studies. 8*, 79–98. Also see Nettle, D. (2005). *Happiness: The science behind your smile*. New York: Oxford University Press.

[4] Norzick, R. (1974). *Anarchy, state and utopia*. New York: Basic Books.

[5] Mill, J. S. (1952/1861). Utilitarianism. In the *Great books of the Western world*. R. M. Hutchins & Adler, M. J. (Eds.), (Chapter 2, pp. 447–457).

the joys that come from art, music, philosophy, religion, and so on. According to Mill, bodily pleasures are appropriate for animals, but humans also seek more noble satisfactions.

Who would argue that pleasure is unimportant? We recognize the value of both the bodily and the higher pleasures, and we agree that they contribute greatly to the quality of life. I have just returned from a large-chain electronics store filled with music videos, CDs, video games, and plasma TVs. The store was jammed with customers in pursuit of pleasure. There is nothing wrong with that, but will they find happiness there? If we are honest with ourselves, I think we will admit that pleasure alone is not enough. A life of drugs, sex, fine wine, and good books is not the ideal for everyone, and probably not the ideal for anyone. It is unlikely that this is what Jefferson had in mind.

HAPPINESS AS WEALTH

A lot of people believe that money brings happiness, and it is not just individuals that hold this view. Many of our most important social institutions have also taken to the pursuit of money. Not long ago I chaired a university committee that included several faculty members and a few prominent citizens from the community. Before one of the meetings, a highly respected judge remarked, "Law used to be a profession, now it is a business." A physician at the table added, "The same is true of medicine."[6] Through the window of our meeting room we could see the future site of a giant campus entertainment complex that now hosts not only university athletic events, but also Madonna, The Wiggles, and *American Idol* – money makers all! Where "giving" used to be the goal of institutions like law, medicine,

[6] I was very surprised to find that Tom Morris, in his book *If Aristotle Ran General Motors* (1997, New York: Owl Book, Henry Holt and Co., p. 52) reports almost exactly the same experience.

politics, and education, "getting" now reigns supreme. Money brings happiness, or so we think.

There can be no doubt that money is important to individual well-being and to the survival of our institutions. It is necessary for essentials such as food and shelter. It gives us security, status, and the option to travel; to hire others to labor for us; and to buy the things we like. At the institutional level, it pays salaries, buys equipment, and enables us to do our jobs.

Money is good! Aristotle thought of it as a "real good" just like food, sleep, and friends. But most of us know, deep down, that wealth doesn't really bring happiness.[7] Money can solve some problems, but how can it relieve the pain of a lost loved one or a failed marriage or an incurable illness? There is ample evidence that the link between money and happiness is really rather weak.

In David Myers' book *The Pursuit of Happiness,*[8] money is discussed in some detail. The research shows that those of us in the developed world are slightly happier than those in poorer nations, and that the very wealthy of the United States experience slightly more happiness than the rest of us. However, these differences are really quite small. Ed Diener, a leading happiness researcher, together with his colleagues[9] studied the well-being of some of America's richest citizens and found them to be only slightly happier than the average citizen. Furthermore, several wealthy people in Diener's sample admitted to being unhappy. Studies of lottery winners lead us to the same conclusion. Those lucky enough to win major jackpots

[7] King, L., & Napa, C. K. (1998). What makes a life good. *Journal of Personality and Social Psychology, 75*, 156–165. King and Napa found that "meaning in life and happiness are essential to the folk concept of the good life, where as money is relatively unimportant."

[8] Myers, D. G. (1992). *The pursuit of happiness: Discovering the pathways to well-being and enduring personal joy.* New York: Harper Collins Publishers.

[9] Diener, E., Horwitz, J., & Emmons, R. (1985). Happiness of the very wealthy. *Social Indicators, 16*, 263–274.

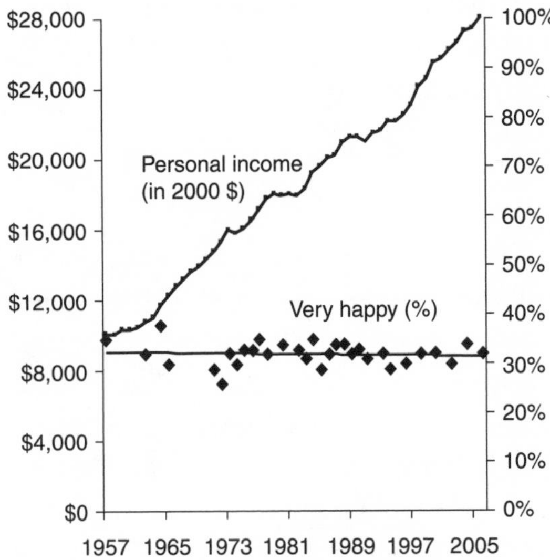

FIGURE 1.1. Personal income and happiness.
Source: Courtesy of David G. Myers. National Opinion Research Center General Social Surveys. Reproduced with permission.

experience very high levels of well-being for about a year but after that, happiness drops back to the previous level.[10]

The graph in Figure 1.1 summarizes fairly well the relationship between wealth and happiness. We see that money makes an important difference to happiness up to a point. After the essentials of food, clothing, shelter, and so on, money doesn't add much to the store. Having too little money can contribute to unhappiness, but if we have enough to cover the necessities of life (BMWs and sailboats are not necessities), it makes relatively little difference. As Myers notes, "well-off is not the same as well-being." Political scientist Robert E.

[10] Brickman, P., Coats, D., & Janoff-Bulman, R. (1978). Lottery winners and accident victims: Is happiness relative? *Journal of Personality and Social Psychology*, *36*, 917–927, and Luter, M. (2007). Book review: Winning a lottery brings no happiness! *Journal of Happiness Studies*, *8*, 155–160.

Lane[11] suggests that the pursuit of money can actually diminish well-being by misdirecting us from the things that really matter, such as family, friends, and community.

RELIGION AS HAPPINESS

God seems to be more important to happiness than money. Myers observes that God provides several important ingredients to our lives. First, we are social animals, and as we congregate and worship together, we find ourselves part of a large, friendly, and protective community. Second, religion offers a sense of purpose and gives meaning to our existence. Myers suggests that we all need something beyond the self to believe in, something to live and die for. Religion grants us a place in the larger scheme of things and gives purpose to our lives. Finally, in God we may find unconditional acceptance and security. Religion tells us that we are not alone and that we can trust in something supremely divine, powerful and caring to watch over us.

For some, the happiness attainable in this life pales in comparison to the eternal joy awaiting us in the next. From the outset, our species has embraced a transcendent world. Traditional societies everywhere accept a spiritual or divine realm beyond the observable. At one time the actions of the skies, the oceans, the fields, and all of nature were inexplicable except in spiritual terms. The powers that moved the world became the early gods and over countless generations these spiritual forces and humans became linked. The roots of monotheism reach back to a sky god, a god higher than all the other spiritual powers, who became formalized in the God of Abraham. Judaism, Christianity, and Islam share the recognition of a single supreme power.[12]

[11] Lane, R. E. (2000). *The loss of happiness in market democracies*. New Haven, CT: Yale University Press.

[12] Armstrong, K. (1993). *A history of God. The 4000 year quest of Judaism, Christianity and Islam*. New York: Ballantine Books.

It was not long after Christianity took hold that it focused on spiritual matters to the exclusion of just about everything else. Saint Augustine, in about 400 A.D., gathered the ideas of earlier thinkers into a formal doctrine that has shaped Christianity for hundreds of years. Augustine contrasted the perfect world of God with the imperfect representations we find in the sensible, everyday world, and urged us to disregard the latter as much as possible.

A good life for Augustine and for the countless generations that followed him during the Middle Ages meant forsaking the world of matter as much as possible. The sensory world, the objective, physical world we know so well was for Augustine something to abhor, while the City of God, the transcendent world, led to salvation and eternal bliss. Happiness was not to be found in earthly possessions or physical pleasures but rather in knowing God. Only religion could bring true happiness.

> Since, then, the supreme good of the city of God is perfect and eternal peace, not such as mortals pass in and out of by birth and death, but the peace of freedom from all evil, in which the immortals ever abide, who can deny that the future life is most blessed, or that, in comparison with it, this life which now we live is most wretched, be it filled with all blessings of body and soul and external things?[13]

Almost a thousand years of devotion to religious and spiritual matters carried Western civilization through what most think of as a very painful time. Most of Europe stagnated as worldly knowledge was forsaken. Cities decayed and poverty enveloped all but the nobility; darkness covered all of Europe.

Enlightenment emerged gradually. A thousand years after the birth of Jesus, the Church initiated the first of a series of Crusades to free the Holy Land from infidels. One of the many unexpected

[13] Augustine, S. (1952). The City of God. In Hutchens, R. M. & Adler, M. J. (Eds.), *Great Books of the Western World*. Book 19, Chapter 20, Encyclopedia Britannica, Inc.

consequences of those Crusades was the rediscovery of Classical Greek writings that had been preserved by Islamic scholars. As the Crusaders returned home to Europe, the ideas of Greek philosophers, especially Aristotle, traveled with them.

Moses Ben Maimon (1135–1204), or Maimonides as he is more commonly known, brought together the teachings of Judaism and Aristotelian philosophy, showing how *reason* and faith together were superior to faith alone. St. Thomas Aquinas (1225–1274) followed Maimonides and laid the foundation of modern Catholicism by recognizing that God gave us senses to know the physical world as well as the spiritual one, furthering the integration of the two. Aquinas brought *faith and reason together* pretty much as they exist in contemporary Christianity.

There were other sources of illumination penetrating the darkness of the Middle Ages. The re-emergence of interest in the natural world encouraged exploration. Columbus sailed to America in 1492; Copernicus (1473–1543) proclaimed the sun, not the earth, as the center of the solar system; Galileo (1564–1642) and Isaac Newton (1642–1727) began the serious investigation of the natural world and laid the foundations of modern science. Newton, while still a believer, found God relatively unimportant for understanding the natural world. God created it but no longer interfered in worldly matters.

With the rebirth of interest in the natural world, the place of man also changed. Early Humanism challenged the early Church's view by claiming that this life *is* important. Eternal bliss may eventually come but in the meantime our earthly lives matter as well. We are both spirit and nature.

HAPPINESS AS FULFILLMENT

The humanists bring us to our final meaning of happiness and the one to which this book is devoted: *Happiness is the fulfillment of human potential.* Happiness is not only about feeling good or being wealthy or being holy. Rather, happiness is fulfilling our inherent possibilities, or, as the U.S. Army commercial says, "be[ing] all that [we] can be."

To live well we humans must, like other creatures, be what we are meant to be. Birds are meant to fly, and to live well they must exercise that potential. Lions are meant to hunt, and if restrained in a zoo they cannot live well. It is not enough to survive and procreate, as some biologists would have it. And the Behaviorists of the mid-twentieth century were wrong too; we are not just pieces of clay to be molded by our environment. John Watson, the founder of the Behavioristic movement in psychology, claimed that if we gave him

> a dozen healthy infants, well formed and my own specified world to bring them up in, ... I'll guarantee to take any one at random and train him to become any type of specialist I might select – a doctor, lawyer, artist, merchant-chief and, yes, even into beggar-man and thief.[14]

Watson misled psychology for decades. Humans are endowed with potentials; we are all latent or actual artists, athletes, teachers, performers, mothers, scientists, and the like. Some of us lack these particular qualities but have been blessed with others. We are not meant to be just one thing or another; each of us has many possibilities. Mother, scientist, friend, artist, and athlete can and should and do co-exist. To the degree that we fulfill our inherent potentials we live well. Two of my children are fairly talented artists, and I have noticed over the years that when they take the time to draw or to paint, they are joyful. But other demands often take precedence. All of us have gifts that we tend to neglect while we devote our lives to other, "more important" tasks. Yes, we must stay attuned to reality, but those who have the discipline to exercise their talents live better. Unexpressed propensities can be damaging. Psychologist Abraham Maslow warns that choosing to ignore your potentials

[14] Watson, J. B. (1924/1970). *Behaviorism*. New York: W.W. Norton; p. 104.

can have dangerous consequences. Carl Rogers suggests we have a genetic blueprint, an array of possibilities that must be fulfilled if we are to have a good life. We will explore their ideas in some detail in Chapter 4.

The fulfillment model makes pleasure only incidental to happiness. Happiness is better viewed as a way of living, not a temporary state that comes and goes. None of us will ever fully realize our potentials but it is a matter of degree; it is about going as far as possible. The more we grow into ourselves the better our lives become. It feels good to exercise or paint or write, or to follow whatever the inclination of our potentials. But the feeling is not the important part; it is only a *by-product of growth*. Good feelings can be used as a guidance device[15] to direct our actions, but good feelings are secondary to the growth upon which happiness depends. It feels good when we do the right thing, when we exercise or master a tennis swing, or act kindly to someone in need. But the correlate of right action should not be the goal. Pleasure is not the cause of happiness but often the by-product of fulfillment. And we must be careful because not all pleasures derive from fulfillment. The good feelings produced by drugs, alcohol, or an extravagant shopping spree can trick and misdirect us. It is actualization, not pleasure, that is the key to a good life.

Happiness has several meanings. It is often thought of as a temporary state, a passing feeling that comes from eating ice cream or seeing a good movie. For some, having money is happiness, and for others it is faith in God. Clearly pleasure, wealth, and spirituality are important elements of every life, but are these what Jefferson intended in the Declaration of Independence? I think not.

Jefferson's life could not be described as fun filled or pleasure seeking. Money was important to him and he abhorred debt, but people

[15] Klinger, E. (1977). *Meaning and void: Inner experience and the incentives in people's lives.* Minneapolis: University of Minnesota Press.

who value money greatly are usually careful with it and don't die broke as the third President did. Further, Jefferson was not a terribly religious person. Many of the founding fathers, including Jefferson, were deists, not devoutly Christian at all. Deists were influenced by the development of Renaissance science that flourished during their time. For the Deist, God was not a personal God at all but rather the creator of an orderly, knowable world. God did not intervene in the affairs of men. It is doubtful that Jefferson's kind of happiness would be tied to such a God.

While we might argue over Jefferson's view of happiness, it is unlikely that he was advocating the pursuit of pleasure, wealth, or God. The founding of America was not far removed from European feudal society where many were confined to serfdom under the heavy hands of feudal lords. These were the conditions that early immigrant Americans sought to escape. They dreamed of a place where they could live safely and freely, and where the pursuit of dreams was possible. The Declaration of Independence guarantees that potential, not heritage, defines one's limits. A new nation needs good citizens. Jefferson may well have realized that the right of each individual to pursue his or her dreams might build a nation worthy of the risk taken by the heroic Founding Fathers. Jefferson could not guarantee a perfect life to everyone, but he may have intended the government to ensure the right of every American to pursue all that his or her natural abilities would allow.

James O'Toole[16] examined Jefferson's personal, underscored copy of Aristotle's *Nichomachean Ethics* in the Library of Congress and concluded that "there is but one way to understand 'the pursuit of happiness' in the Declaration: *It refers to the process of realizing one's full potential.*"

[16] O'Toole, J. (2005). *Creating the good life: Applying Aristotle's wisdom to find meaning and happiness.* New York: Rodale. See especially pp. 28 and 50.

From our point of view then, happiness is not a series of transient pleasures or fabulous wealth, and it's not dependent on religious beliefs. The kind of happiness to which we refer continues even when we feel bad. The happiness discussed in this book is a way of living that enables us to fulfill potentials and move toward a good human life.

2

Happiness as Fulfillment

> The great law of culture is: Let each become all that he was created capable of being.
>
> Thomas Carlyle, *Critical and Miscellaneous Essays*, 1827

The legal right to the pursuit of happiness probably means that Americans are granted the freedom to become all that they might become. While America embraced this wonderful thought at its founding, it was hardly a new idea. Aristotle proposed it almost 2,500 years ago, but the notion of fulfillment has rarely been made explicit or become very popular. It goes by different names such as self-realization or actualization as well as fulfillment, and it is a rather abstract and difficult idea. It is probably easier to think of happiness in terms of pleasure or money or goods – a leisurely vacation, winning the lottery, or a nice home.

I want to explore the idea of fulfillment further but before doing so, it might be helpful to take a brief look at the life of its originator.

Born in Macedonia, just north of what is now Greece, Aristotle was the son of the King's physician. At the age of about 17 Aristotle traveled to Athens to study at Plato's Academy. He remained with Plato for about 20 years until his mentor's death. While Aristotle and Plato had much in common, they did differ on one very important issue. For Plato, truth was to be found in a transcendent world of ideas that is accessed through reason. Aristotle, while accepting the importance of reason, gave much more importance to the natural, physical world. He was really the first scientist, proposing that knowledge comes through observation of the material world. Aristotle's view of happiness was influenced by the importance he gave to the natural world.

In 343 B.C., Aristotle was invited by King Phillip of Macedonia to tutor his son and therefore returned to his birthplace to mentor the boy later to be known as Alexander the Great. Following his teaching position at the palace, Aristotle returned to Athens and opened his own academy which he called the Lyceum. After the death of Alexander, anti-Macedonian feelings in Athens grew very intense and forced Aristotle to return to Macedonia where he died in 322 B.C.

Aristotle's many contributions continue to influence Western civilization to this day. Among his writings are essays and books on logic, physics, meteorology, metaphysics, the soul, the senses, dreams, memory and sleep, aging, ethics, politics, rhetoric, and poetics. Furthermore, it is believed that only a fraction of his writings actually survived. Aristotle was truly one of the most brilliant and prolific minds the world has known.

The book you are reading was inspired by and based upon Aristotle's *Nicomachean Ethics.*[1] Ethics meant something very different in Ancient Greece than what it means today. Ethics now usually refers to rules of conduct that govern professions or social behavior. We have professional ethics in medicine, law, education, religion, and so on, and we often judge actions as ethical or unethical. In Ancient Greece, however, ethics was concerned with the problem of how to live. Aristotle called living well *eudaimonia* (pronounced *u-day-monia*). While there is no adequate English translation of the term, it generally refers to what we now call a good human life or just plain happiness.

[1] Aristotle, *The Nicomachean Ethics*. D. Ross (trans.). (1986). New York: Oxford University Press.

As someone interested in the natural world, Aristotle used an acorn to illustrate the ideas of fulfillment and happiness. An acorn has within it the potential to become an oak tree. Inherent in the acorn is the form or pattern of "oaktreeness." It can never become a frog or an eagle, only an oak tree. Similarly, the fertilized egg within the soon-to-be mother has the potential to become a boy or girl but not a fox or a rosebush. Living things have potentials, possibilities, patterns, or forms inherent within them. "Oaktreenes" is a pattern within the acorn. Man- or womanhood is a pattern within the human zygote. And within the zygote are possibilities of athlete, artist, scientist, mother, friend, and so on. We are potentially many things in varying amounts. Just as the acorn strives for growth, so do we. Living things share the urge to "become." Potentials may be thought of as needs in pursuit of satisfaction. Aristotle suggests that we spend our lives in pursuit. We must navigate the natural world to fulfill our human needs just as the acorn must draw its nourishment from the soil and sunlight. The acorn reaches to the sky and we pursue our fulfillment, "*eudaimonia*," or happiness.

We will learn more about fulfillment in Chapter 4 but this is the basic idea. Our kind of happiness is not feeling good, being rich, or having stuff; rather, it is a way of living. Pleasure comes and goes, but our kind of happiness is lasting; it's there even when we are hurting and when life is unkind to us. As long as we are in pursuit, moving forward, developing, and fulfilling our potential, we have a good human life: *eudaimonia* or happiness.

Most of us have learned that what brings happiness to one person may not satisfy another, and we may conclude from this that happiness is unique to each person. If this were true, no general explanation of happiness would be possible. But, as you can see from Aristotle's thinking, although potentials may differ among people – one person might be a musician and another an athlete – all are in pursuit. People can be happy doing different things. Differences between people are allowed!

Bev Karu, our departmental secretary, once gave me a poster with an anonymous quotation that read "Forget about the pursuit of happiness. That way lies grief. Concentrate on the happiness of pursuit." Wonderful! The "happiness of pursuit.": there is no real destination or finish line, there is only the journey. Traveling *is* happiness. Growing *is* happiness. Fulfilling potentials *is* happiness.

3

Aristotle's Ethics

Reason is God's crowning gift to man.
Sophocles (496–406 B.C.)

There are 54 volumes in the *Great Books of the Western World* series edited by Robert Maynard Hutchins and Mortimer Adler. Charles Darwin's writings are found in Volume 49 and Sigmund Freud has the last word in Volume 54. Some people may take these two intellectual giants for granted and others may doubt their sanity, but all must admit that Darwin's and Freud's inclusion with the likes of Plato, Copernicus, Chaucer, Shakespeare, and Newton counts for something. Darwin and Freud have much in common, but from the perspective of this book, one shared idea stands out: Humankind is something less than divine. To put it even more strongly, humans are very much like animals. Pointing out our irrationality is Freud's major contribution. He reminds us that our major motives derive from irrational sex and aggression urges which often cause us to make bad decisions and to misbehave. If you doubt the influence of sex and aggression motives, just turn on the TV tonight.

When these urges lead us to irrational behavior, we frequently excuse ourselves by proclaiming "I'm only human." The idea of our inherent irrationality is very much ingrained in us. Darwin says that we're very much like animals and Freud says that we are driven by unconscious motives that make life really interesting but also very troublesome. One can expect only so much from our species; we are, after all, only human.

The Darwinian/Freudian views of humanity have not always been popular. In fact, throughout much of history, we find just the opposite to be true. For the Ancient Greeks, our ability to think, to reason, and to understand separated us from the animals. Reason was our *ergon*, our unique quality, our distinctive human function. Certainly humans can be irrational at times, but we should always try to use our ability to reason – it is what we do best. Lions may be strong and ferocious, but we can think.

Before the Ancient Greek civilization, people everywhere believed that the world was run by supernatural forces, by gods who controlled the oceans, the sky, the hunt, good and bad fortune. The Greeks, however, while giving their due to the gods, argued that the world is governed by reasonable principles or natural law. And we humans, using our *ergon*, can comprehend the world and its laws. This was the beginning of science; today we predict the weather, repair a broken body, and send spaceships to Mars. Reason can be much more effective than pleading to the gods. Understanding the principles that run the world allows us to act with foresight and, to a considerable degree, to make things happen.

Remember Aristotle's syllogisms:

> All men are mortal.
> Socrates is a man.
> Therefore …
> Socrates will die.

Other creatures can't reason like that. We can think and understand. It is our *ergon* to reason, that's what makes us human. Aristotle believed that the world is an orderly place and that we have the capacity to understand it. In fact, we *need* to know and *need* to understand. It is a human potential that seeks fulfillment.

Aristotle combined the centrality of human reason with the idea of fulfillment to develop a formula for living. In the *Nichomachean Ethics* he described that formula. Today we think of ethics as a set of rules to be followed, but the word *ethics* is actually related to the Greek word *ethos*, which refers to something like "habits of living." Aristotle's *Ethics* is really a book about the habits we need to live a good human life.

I have tried to put Aristotle's ideas into the language of today and to share his formula for a good life with those who might otherwise never encounter his writings. Aristotle is tough to read and difficult to understand. For almost 2,500 years his books and essays have been the subject of intense study, yet we still don't fully understand much of his writings. Aristotle's *Ethics* seems a bit like Einstein's relativity theory. Although relativity theory was developed 100 years ago, even today only a few understand it fully. Aristotle's *Ethics* is similarly difficult.

In a nutshell, Aristotle suggests that with the help of reason we can fulfill our potentials. Fulfilling potentials is the key to living well, to happiness, and to what Aristotle called *eudaimonia*. We are not talking about the happiness of good feelings that come and go, but rather the happiness of a full and meaningful human life. In the remainder of this chapter, I will outline the major ideas of Aristotle's *Ethics* in a language that is, hopefully, more friendly to the modern reader.

GOODS

Just as an acorn needs sunlight, water, and nutrients from the soil to grow into a stately oak, there are things that humans need in order to actualize. We need what Aristotle called *real goods*. Many real goods are easily identifiable. Everyone recognizes the need for food, clothing, and shelter, but the arts, music, and literature are also important for the development of our higher human faculties. We may need a car to commute to work so that we can earn a living. Money is also a real good because it buys so many of the things we need. Family and friends are real goods because we are social creatures and need the love and support of others. Aristotle didn't spend a lot of time writing about real goods, probably because he thought that most of us were already familiar with them.

I should mention here that not all goods are real goods. Many of the things we pursue do not change our lives. A lot of things give pleasure but have nothing to do with fulfillment. You might need a watch to tell time but no one needs a Rolex. You might need a car to get to work but no one needs a Rolls Royce. We will address this issue again in a later chapter, but we should note here that many of the things we pursue are what Aristotle called *apparent goods.* Apparent goods give pleasure but don't have anything to do with the fulfillment of potentials. Let me be clear here: There is nothing wrong with pleasure or the apparent goods that bring it about. But, we should recognize an important distinction. Real goods improve your life; apparent goods give pleasure but do not improve your life. We *need* real goods; we *want* apparent goods. I own a couple of Rolexes (one a 1946 model given to me by a friend, and the other, from the 1960s, was a birthday present from Brenda, my wife). I enjoyed fixing the older one and get some pleasure from occasionally wearing them. But they haven't changed my life one bit; I recognize them for what they are – apparent goods. Apparent goods are fine, but we should be able to tell the difference between them and the really important things that move us toward fulfillment, the real goods.

VIRTUE

Virtue is a Latin word that has changed in meaning over the ages. When we see or hear the word now, it may bring to mind ideas like chastity or good deeds, but as Aristotle used it (actually the Greek word for virtue is *arête*), it referred to something quite different. Virtue, as Aristotle used it in the *Ethics*, means *excellence.*

Although science as we know it today was almost 2,000 years into the future, the Ancient Greeks created a world view that made science possible. They thought of the world as an orderly place that we could come to know and understand. *Logos*, or *reason/rule,* prevails in the world and, given our *ergon,* we have the ability to understand the reasonableness that fills the world. Vanier[1] put it nicely: "logos is a light that enables us to contemplate, understand, reason, order, name, control and regulate." The world is reasonable and we can be too. When we reason well, we participate in *logos*.

Because the world is an orderly and reasonable place, we can *do* well if we *reason* well. *Virtue*, excellent thinking, or the right use of reason helps us get the goods we need to actualize potentials. *Virtue refers to the correct use of reason to obtain what we need for a good human life.*

There are a couple of different kinds of virtuous thinking that we should identify. First, according to Aristotle, there are general principles or truths that we need to understand. For example, we have to know what a good life is before we can go about trying to build one. Do comfort, ease, and luxury make a good life? If not, what does? The point is, we need to understand certain principles before we can act reasonably. Further, we must choose to follow some of those principles. Most would agree that a life filled with drugs, crime, and disregard for the rights of others would not make us very happy. But what principles shall we choose to guide us? We must know the principles, understand them, and choose from among them. Aristotle calls this kind of knowledge *intellectual virtue.*

[1] Vanier, J. (2001). *A guide to a good life: Happiness, Aristotle for the new century.* New York: Arcade Publishing, pp. 18 and 158.

Knowing, however, is not enough. *Logos* is essential but it alone is not sufficient to build a good human life. Aristotle's thinking differs in an important way from his predecessors Socrates and Plato, who maintained that the way we live depends almost entirely on the way we think. For Plato, *logos* – reason and thinking – was much more important than the world of actions. For Aristotle, the *use* of reason was just as important as reason itself. We might know what a good life is but be clueless about how to get it. We might know and embrace the right ends but lack the proper means to achieve them. It is possible to know that we need friendship and love but lack the skills to fulfill these needs. Both a worthy destination and a means of travel are essential.

We must learn how to *do,* as well as how to think. Aristotle used the term *moral virtue* to describe "doing knowledge." Moral virtue is the ability to correctly *use* the *logos* we have. We need to understand what friendship and fairness mean, but we also have to learn how to make friends and to be fair. Moral virtue refers to behavior and to the development of good habits and efficient, moral actions that assist in fulfilling potential. Vanier summarizes it this way:

> There are two things in which all well-being consists: one of them is the choice of the right end and aim of action, the other the discovery of the actions which are means toward it.

EMOTION

To Aristotle, the word "soul" meant something different than it means today. The term had no religious connection but simply referred to the "form of living things." All living things, therefore, have a soul; it is the essence of life. The soul of humankind differs from the soul of animals, however, in that our soul includes an intellectual or rational function. Plants and spiders have a soul but lack the power of reason.

The human soul has two major divisions: the rational part, which we have already discussed, and the irrational part, which includes desires and emotions. Sigmund Freud focused primarily on the importance of the irrational functions. But desire and emotion were important to Aristotle too, because they drive behavior. Without desire or emotions such as anger, sadness, and love, we would have no motivation and would be inert and unable to act on our own. Desire and emotion propel us, for good or for ill; they drive behavior.

Unbridled desire and emotion can be dangerous. Uncontrolled lust, anger, or sadness can be harmful to ourselves and to others. If I cannot control my anger, I'm likely to get into serious trouble. If my grief becomes overwhelming, I may want to end my life. Desire and emotion are irrational but they do affect our behavior; they are the sources of energy that power our actions. But – and this is the important part – desire and emotion do not act in isolation to produce behavior. They can be joined with reason to create rational action. *Desire and emotion are not rational but can be combined with reason.* Our fears can be controlled and our desires can be moderated by thinking. We do it all the time; for example, we suffer a defeat but *think* that we can recover, and then the defeat does not seem so devastating. Love fails and sadness begins, but reason saves the day. We know in our heads, if not in our hearts, that life goes on even in sadness.

Virtue includes both emotion and thinking, that is, desire and emotion and the moderating effects of reason. So, while emotion is irrational, it is necessary for action and leads to right action when overseen by good thinking. In a more modern interpretation, Aristotle proposes, quite correctly, I think, that when motivation (desire/emotion) is directed by good intellectual processes, good, adaptive behavior results.

Veatch[2] summarizes this idea very nicely: "morals and ethics are to be regarded as involving no more than learning and knowing

[2] Veatch, H. B. (1962). *Rational man: A modern interpretation of Aristotle's Ethics.* Indiana: University of Indiana Press, pp. 90–91.

how to bring our intelligence and understanding to bear upon our passions and desires." We will have a lot more to say about this part of Aristotle's theory in the chapter on emotion.

THE GOLDEN MEAN

I doubt that my father ever read Aristotle's *Ethics*, but he did refer to the *golden mean* quite often. He used to say "everything in moderation" and lived quite close to that ideal. Although "everything in moderation" is similar to Aristotle's *golden mean*, it is a bit of an oversimplification. Aristotle's words actually are: "virtue is a mean, with regard to what is best and right and extreme." Let's briefly explore this thought.

We noted earlier that, in order to fulfill potentials, we need real goods such as food, shelter, money, friends, and so on. But here Aristotle gets a bit more specific. Of course food is a real good, but how much food is really good? If we have too little our health might be ruined, but too much food can also be harmful. There is a right amount of food for each of us. The same can be said of most of the real goods we need. Too little money is detrimental to our well-being, yet having too much can also be a heavy burden. I remember reading a quotation by Bill Gates upon the birth of his first child. When asked if he was going to leave his fortune to his new daughter he replied, "I would never *burden* her with that much money." Too much or too little of almost anything can be harmful: too many bills, too much garden to maintain, too many – or too few – social obligations, too many mouths to feed, too few loved ones to care for.

If you think about it, I am sure you will agree that there is a right amount of almost everything needed for a good life. I remember a commencement speaker who was serving as an ambassador to a Latin nation. He came from a poor family from the barrio but worked his way up in the political community and experienced considerable success in his career. He described the life of an ambassador and the luxuries he was experiencing, how each morning a limosine would pick him up and then deliver him back home at the end of the day. He told the students how wonderful his life now was and urged them to work hard, succeed, and remember that "You can never get too much of a good thing." Well, not according to Aristotle! Too much of even a great thing such as money can be harmful. There is evidence that many major lottery winners are broke within three years and wish that they had never won.[3] I recall a young woman who appeared on television and described how she had lost all of her friends and most of her family when she won the lottery. They all wanted money! She had too much and when she refused to give her fortune away, they rejected her. Too little and too much of just about anything is not good. The virtuous person who thinks well and chooses the right amount of what is needed selects the *golden mean*: the right amount.

But Aristotle also recognized that each of us is different. The right amount of food for you might be too little or too much for me. There is no specific, identifiable amount of any good that can be prescribed. Rather, Aristotle observed, the *golden mean* is always relative to the person: "Virtue, then, is a state of character concerned with choice, lying in a mean, i.e. *the mean relative to us.*" We will explore this idea further in a later chapter, but for now it is important to note that virtue requires us to choose wisely and to seek the right amount of the goods we need. Fulfillment does not mean "overflowing." And we must remember that what may be good for one person is not necessarily good for another. There is no one amount of any good that is right for everyone. Grandfathers and grandchildren rarely need the same amount of anything! As we reach adulthood, however, we must be responsible for selecting the right amount for ourselves. To live well we need to choose well, to find our *golden means.*

[3] See www.lottoreport.com/sadbuttrue.htm

ACTUALIZATION AND THE COMMUNITY

Aristotle's ideas about actualization have often been criticized for promoting selfishness.[4] Some claim that concern with individual fulfillment neglects the needs of others. Some philosophers suggest that to be ethical we must put others before ourselves. The community can only survive when individual needs are subordinated to the general welfare.

Freud emphasized the inevitable conflict between the needs of the individual and the needs of the community in a book entitled *Civilization and Its Discontents*,[5] suggesting that to be civilized or to be tamed by the community necessarily causes unhappiness in the individual. But for Aristotle ethics and politics serve the *same* end: a good life for both. Good people make a good community!

Following the *Nichomachean Ethics*, Aristotle wrote *Politics*.[6] In it he stated that the purpose of the *polis* or the community and the purpose of virtue are the same. Both are directed toward the actualization of the individual citizen, both are means to growth and fulfillment. "The purpose of the city is thus to enable its citizens to live a life of virtue or excellence." Virtue is not compatible with selfishness. People with good judgment, who choose well and live well, are not in conflict with each other. Both virtue and the *polis* exist for the sake of the good life and they do not at all need to oppose one another. Virtue creates good citizens and happy people, and these same persons make up the *polis*. The ideal *polis* is a community of fulfilled people attending to both their own needs and the needs of others. Virtue is good for the individual

4 Milton, J. (2002). *The road to Malpsychia: Humanistic psychology and our discontents*. San Francisco: Encounter Books.

5 Freud, S. (1962/1930). *Civilization and its discontents*. New York: W.W. Norton & Co. Inc.

6 Aristotle. *Politics. The philosophy of Aristotle*. (1963). Translated by A.E. Wardman and J. L. Creed, New York: Mentor Book, New American Library.

and for the community. A fulfilled individual, to Aristotle, is also a good citizen, a member of the *polis,* enhancing it as he improves himself.

We can capture the essence of Aristotle's *Ethics* with just a few ideas. Barring unforeseen accidents or bad luck, a person can know the joys of a good life if he or she manages to acquire the real goods needed for fulfillment. Virtue, which combines emotion and desire with reason, is essential to getting the right amount of any good. It is essential to finding the *golden mean.* Individual fulfillment is not selfish or contrary to the best interests of the community but just the opposite; it enhances the *polis* and the lives of all citizens.

4

Actualization: Psychological Views

> If you deliberately plan on being less than you are capable of being, then I warn you that you'll be unhappy for the rest of your life.
>
> Abraham Maslow[1]

ABRAHAM MASLOW

Abraham Maslow (1908–1970) was one of the first psychologists to embrace Aristotle's idea of fulfillment. It was Maslow who began the Humanistic tradition in modern psychology and it was he who suggested that the discipline concerns itself with psychological wellness and not just misery, which had been the focus of so much earlier psychology. Unlike the Freudians who emphasized our irrational sexual and aggressive tendencies, Maslow saw human nature as good and inclusive of noble motives. While our basic human needs require some satisfaction, there is also a side of us that longs for beauty, justice, love, and other *metamotives*, as Maslow calls them. These can also be thought of as potentials in need of fulfillment.

The commonly recognized needs such as hunger, security, friendship, and so on are referred to as *deficiency motives*. The deficiency motives consume most of our lives but the fortunate among us are able to fulfill these and go on to higher levels of functioning, to what (Maslow calls the pursuit of value and truth. *Metamotives*)

[1] Maslow, A. (1971/1982). *The Farther Reaches of Human Nature*. New York: Penguin Books, p. 35. With permission from Ms. Ann Kaplan.

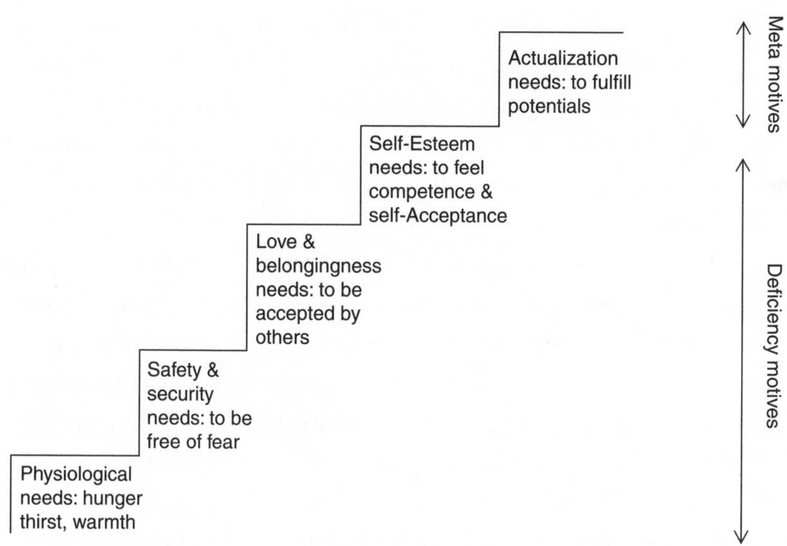

FIGURE 4.1. Abraham Maslow's hierarchy of needs.

such as these emerge only after the lower-level needs have been sufficiently, but not necessarily completely, satisfied. For Maslow, then, the best part of our nature does not express itself until the more basic human needs are at least somewhat satisfied. Although human nature does include the traits we so admire such as fairness, beauty, and compassion, these usually express themselves most fully when we are far along the developmental ladder. Let's look a little more closely at Maslow's view of human motivation which is summarized in Figure 4.1.[2]

There is a *hierarchy of needs*.[3] When a lower-level need is sufficiently satisfied, the next level emerges and then the next and so on, until the fifth or highest level, the *need of self-actualization*, emerges. It is at this level that the best in us appears.

[2] Adapted from Petri, H. L. & Govern, J. M. (2004). *Motivation: Theory, research, and applications*. Belmont, CA: Thomson/Wadsworth.

[3] Maslow, A. (1970/1954). *Motivation and personality*. New York: Harper & Row Publishers.

The lowest and most basic human needs are the *physiological needs*. Until we have enough food to eat and clothes to keep warm we are not likely to be very interested in art, world peace, or global warming. But if we are able to satisfy our most essential physiological needs, we can move to the second level of deficiency motives, which Maslow calls the need for *safety and security*. On the battlefield, in dark alleys where the homeless reside, in the prison where aggression lurks around every corner, there is fear, worry, and apprehension. Children who are, for one reason or another, deprived of proper parenting and security cannot develop properly and will not become all that they might. Too many on the planet suffer the deprivation of safety and security and live in fear. It is a basic human need to feel safe and free from danger, but in so many that need goes unmet. If people are preoccupied with protecting themselves they cannot become and cannot actualize. They can not fulfill their human potential.

We are social animals. We need others just as we need food and safety. Maslow called our social need *belongingness and love*. It is a fundamental requirement to be loved by others, to be a part of a social unit such as a family, gang, church, fraternity, fan club, or sports team. William James, the brilliant and ever so insightful Victorian psychologist/philosopher, remarked on our need to be with our kind:

> No more fiendish punishment could be devised, were such a thing possible, than that one should be turned loose in society and remain absolutely unnoticed by all the members thereof. If no one turned round when we entered, answered when we spoke, or minded what we did, but if every person we met 'cut us dead,' and acted as if we were non-existing things, a kind of rage and impotent despair would ere long well up in us, from which the cruelest bodily tortures would be a relief.[4]

[4] James, W. (1969/1892). *Psychology: Briefer course*. London: Collier-Macmillan Ltd.

We wonder why so many of our children form clicks, clubs, or gangs even though these may be hurtful to others and even to the children themselves. Their need to be loved, to belong, and to be accepted is just as real and just as powerful as their passions.

If we are lucky enough to fulfill our need for love and belongingness, we move upward to the need for *self-esteem*. Not only do we need to be well regarded by others, we need to think well of ourselves, too. Our need to be accepted now evolves into the desire for respect, recognition, and status. Isn't it interesting that it is fine for us to dislike someone, but if that person should dislike us in return we become uncomfortable? We need others to think well of us so that we can think well of ourselves. Today we have a variety of mechanisms to bestow honor upon ourselves. An Academy Award or Emmy, a trophy or certificate, our name in the paper or in the post office – sometimes it doesn't matter, as long as we are noticed. Recognition boosts our self-esteem.

Maslow suggests these four deficiency needs are hierarchical, that is, the lower-order needs come first and demand satisfaction before we can move on to the next level. When the homeless beg for food and fear for their lives, they are not likely to be concerned with what you might think of them or even whether they are accepted by their fellow down-and-outers on the street. They are motivated only by the prepotent desire to have enough to eat and to be secure for the night.

Providing that one is able to adequately (but not necessarily completely) satisfy all four levels of the deficiency needs, he or she will be one of the few among us to move on to what Maslow calls the *self-actualization* need. This level of motivation is very different from the lower-order deficiency needs because there is no emptiness or "need" as such. The mature individual who travels this far on the road to fulfillment is driven, according to Maslow, not by needs but rather by *values*. That person acts not because something is lacking (such as food or love) or because of self-interest, but because of principles and the belief that it is the right thing to do. That person's motives are found in a commitment to truth, beauty, and justice rather than in some kind of personal deficit. The self-actualizing person is motivated by noble and selfless principle and by beliefs and values, not by deficiencies. We all have the potential to express our goodness and to be what Maslow calls a *self-actualizing person*, but few of us attain such heights because it usually takes a lifetime just to satisfy the deficiency needs.

As a graduate student, along with most of my fellow students, I largely dismissed Maslow's ideas because they were less than scientific and lacked sufficient empirical support. Even today there is relatively little research on Maslow's hierarchy and his view of the self-actualizing person.[5] However, as the years have passed, I find more and more value in Maslow's observations. Needs, in the main, do appear to be hierarchical and the truly mature individual does seem to be driven by principles and values more than by deficiencies. Although it is rather discouraging to believe that the best in us cannot flower until the lower needs have been satisfied and that most of the world's inhabitants have a very long way to go, there is some comfort in knowing what is needed. Self-actualization or Aristotle's *eudaimonia* may indeed be beyond the reach of many but an understanding of the idea just might make a world of difference.

Adding a little clarity to the picture of the healthy, happy, and mature person, Maslow conducted a methodologically less-than-perfect study of actualizing people, both living and historical figures. I will be brief here but should the reader wish to pursue

[5] Wicker, F. W., Brown, G., Wiehe, J. A., Hagen, A. S., & Reed, J. L. (1993). On reconsidering Maslow: An examination of the deprivation/domination proposition. *Journal of Research in Personality, 27*, 118–133. These authors suggest that Maslow's motivational theory is very difficult to empirically test and that past attempts have serious methodological flaws. Their findings lend some support to Maslow's ideas on the relationship between deprivation and dominance of motives. Hagerty, M. R. (1999) Testing Maslow's hierarchy of needs: National quality-of-life across time. *Social Indicators Research, 46*, 249–271 finds evidence for Maslow's sequencing of needs at the level of whole nations.

the topic further, I recommend Maslow's book, *Motivation and Personality.*[6] Chapter 11 is devoted to "Self-Actualizing People: A Study of Psychological Health."

The first attribute found in Maslow's sample of actualizing people was *more efficient perception of reality.* He found in these people "an unusual ability to detect the spurious, the fake, the dishonest ...and in general to judge people correctly and efficiently. ... They are far ... more apt to perceive what is there rather than their own wishes, hopes, fears, anxieties." These actualizing people do not need to distort their perceptions to protect themselves; they see the bad in the world as well as the good and they are open rather than closed to reality. They see themselves accurately with faults as well as strengths, and they see others for what they are. In sum, self-actualizing people are not defensive and, therefore, can accept the world for what it is.

A second characteristic of self-actualizing persons is *spontaneity and naturalness.* Briefly, these people are honest with themselves and with others. They don't need to pretend to be something they are not. They do not try to impress others but are content to be what they are. They are self-assured but not arrogant; they are confident but not offensively so.

Third, Maslow found his subjects to be *problem centered.* They are "focused on problems outside themselves ... they are problem centered rather than ego centered." Actualizing people largely have met their deficiency needs and now they are working for the benefit of others or in science, the arts, philanthropy, and so on for the benefit of mankind in general. A quote from Albert Einstein, one of Maslow's self-actualizing subjects, summarizes this quality: "The true value of a human being is determined primarily by the measure and the sense in which he has attained liberation from the self."[7]

[6] Maslow, A. (1970/1954). *Motivation and personality.* New York: Harper & Row Publishers.

[7] Einstein, A. (1978). *Ideas and opinions.* New York: Dell Publishing Co., p. 23.

Fourth, actualizing persons tend to enjoy solitude and privacy, and stand relatively detached from the fray. Most avoid the limelight when they are able. These people often remain rather aloof and above the battle, appearing to some as cold and snobbish. However, according to Maslow, they simply remain self-directed and self-governing, unappreciative of popular culture, TV advertisers, and the latest fads. Crowds, power, and popularity are just not very important to these people. They tend to be *detached* from many of the things that interest the majority of us and prefer just a few friends with whom they can share their interests and views. I'm reminded of another statement from Einstein on this topic:

> My passionate sense of social justice and social responsibility has always contrasted oddly with my pronounced lack of need for direct contact with other human beings and human communities. I am truly a "lone traveler" and have never belonged to my country, my home, my friends, or even my immediate family, with my whole heart. … One becomes sharply aware, but without regret, of the limits of mutual understanding and consonance with other people.[8]

Elsewhere Einstein expresses deep regret over his dismal performance as husband and father, which might be explained, in this context, as an admirable quality taken to the extreme.

Despite a sense of remoteness from others and the world, Maslow notes that his subjects tend to have a wonderful sense of appreciation of the simple things in life: "For such people, even the casual workaday, moment to moment business of living can be thrilling, exciting and ecstatic." They do not take for granted, as so many of us seem to do, the blessings of each day but "appreciate, freshly and naively, the basic goods of life with awe, pleasure, wonder and even ecstasy" (p.163).

There are other traits that Maslow finds in actualizing people but hopefully we have demonstrated that Maslow's "happiness" is

[8] Ibid, p. 21.

far from simple enjoyment and is something much deeper and more profound. And we must be careful not to take Maslow's description too seriously, recognizing as did he that it is only a beginning to the mystery of actualization.

CARL ROGERS

Carl Rogers (1902–1987) was also a Humanistic psychologist who built upon Aristotle's idea of actualization. Rogers claimed that all living things have an *actualizing tendency,* a force to develop, grow, and fulfill potential. For Rogers hunger, love, and achievement are all just specific examples of the fundamental *need to become.* "The actualizing tendency can be thwarted, but it cannot be destroyed without destroying the organism." Rogers describes his recollection of a potato bin in the basement of his boyhood home. He remembers a potato far below the basement window that shot up pale white sprouts two or three feet in length as they reached toward the distant light. These were so unlike the healthy green shoots of potatoes planted in the soil.

> they were, in their bizarre, futile growth, a sort of desperate expression of the directional tendency I have been describing. They would never become a plant, never mature, never fulfill their real potentiality. But under the most adverse circumstances they were striving to become. Life would not give up, even if it could not flourish.[9]

Rogers likens these pitiful potatoes to patients he has seen in the back wards of mental hospitals who also are striving in the only way available to them. Rogers concludes: "To us the results may seem bizarre and futile, but they are life's desperate attempt to become itself."

The circumstances under which many of us live may be similar to the basement of Rogers' childhood home. The deprived potato, like

[9] Rogers, C. R. (1961). *On becoming a person: A therapist view of psychotherapy.* Boston: Houghton Mifflin.

Aristotle's acorn, has needs. Both the acorn and the potato require sunshine, nutrients, and water for their healthy development. And, like these simple plants, we humans also have requirements.

Rogers suggests that the fulfillment of two particular needs beyond the basic needs are especially important to well-being. The first is *unconditional positive regard.* That's a term Rogers uses for acceptance. He notes that most of us receive *conditional positive regard* or acceptance depending on how well we conform to others' expectations. It is not at all unusual for parents to convey to their child, "I accept you when you behave properly," or "I love you when you meet my requirements." If the child goes to college, gets a high-paying job, marries, and has beautiful children, and so on then the child is good. In other words, acceptance is conditional upon fulfilling other peoples' expectations. When this happens, as it so often does, Rogers claims that we cannot become ourselves. We are too busy becoming what others want us to be. Our potentials are not causal; rather, the expectancies and requirements of parents, teachers, and society in general become the primary motivational forces that guide the behavior. But when we live as others want, we usually fail ourselves. I'm reminded here once again of William James, the early twentieth century philosopher/psychologist of whom I am so fond. James wanted most of all to be an artist but his father thought that was unbecoming to a gentleman of that period, so James became a physician/scientist as his father wished.[10] Although James was highly successful in many ways, I don't think he was ever a truly happy man. James experienced serious depressive periods throughout his life and although he produced one of the world's greatest psychological works, James was never pleased by its contents or its acceptance and instant popularity. It is not unreasonable to think that James was a victim of Rogers' *conditional positive*

[10] Bjork, D. W. (1983). *The compromised scientist: William James in the development of American psychology.* New York: Columbia University Press.

regard. He pleased those around him but was unable to be what he truly wished.

I have a small sign in my study that Brenda, my wife of 48 years, found in a Louisiana antique shop. It reads "Be what you is, because if you is what you ain't, then you ain't what you is." How prophetic! "Be what you is"! Being what you are not, at the end of the day, will make you unhappy.

The second requirement for actualization noted by Rogers is "*organismic listening, or trusting*." In order "to be what you is" you must know "what you is," that is, you must have some consciousness of your potentials. You must know yourself. That was Socrates' first commandment ... *know thyself*. How many of us really know ourselves this way? Do you ever get the feeling that you know a few close friends better than you know yourself? *Ogranismic listening* is Rogers' term for truly paying attention to your needs, hopes, and dreams. It is not just a cognitive, intellectual, brainy, activity but rather one heavily weighted with emotion. Your whole body feels and knows. When you are anxious, anxiousness flows through your being – in your body movements, your speech, your gait, and even your eye movements. A good clinical psychologist can read your mind by attending to your body. We ought do the same: attend to our organism and our whole being. Listen to what our body is telling us about our wishes, dreams, and potentials. To be yourself you must know yourself, and to know yourself you must "listen."

For those who are intent on pleasing others, *organismic listening* is very difficult to do. We look outside, not inside, for direction. We wish to please others, not ourselves. Many of us have become accustomed to seeking guidance from family, books, TV, or friends, and don't even know how to "listen to ourselves." Eric Fromm[11] explains how we are alienated or separated from ourselves. We fill our time with leisure activities, TV, working, and anything we can find to

[11] Fromm, E. (1955). *The sane society*. Greenwich, CT: Fawcett Publications, Inc.

avoid looking deeply within. Ours seems to be an externally driven culture. We fail to understand the wisdom within us. Rogers urges us to change and wants us to know ourselves so that we can know our potentials and can work at their actualization. "Know what you is so that you can work at being what you is."

To summarize Carl Rogers' rendition of Aristotle: We need to be accepted by others for what we are and we need to accept others for what they are. Not all of us are good with computers or have the potential to be a rocket scientist. We all have potentials but these differ from person to person. We need not approve all behaviors, but we need to respect our differences and accept ourselves. Rogers calls this *unconditional positive regard.*

We also need *organismic listening.* We need to take the time to learn about ourselves. It isn't necessary to meditate or to withdraw to a deserted island to do *organismic listening.* You can look inside yourself when you are doing the dishes, raking the lawn, or driving home from work. It's not easy but it is essential. Explore yourself like you would another that you cared about. As Socrates said, "know thyself."

Variations of the Humanistic model of the good human life now appear in the theory and research of some contemporary psychologists such as Carol Ryff. Ryff and colleagues[12] have a view conceptually similar to Maslow's and Rogers' and converges the thoughts of several philosophers and Humanistic psychologists into six dimensions, which they suggest characterize a eudaimonic life: (1) *self-acceptance*, (2) *positive relationships*, (3) *personal growth*, (4) *life purpose*, (5) *environmental mastery*, and (6) *autonomy*. The overlap of

[12] Ryff, C. D. (1989). Happiness is everything or is it? Explorations on the meaning of psychological well-being. *Journal of Personality and Social Psychology*, 57 (6), 1069–1081. Also, Ryff, C. D., & Singer, B. H. (1998). The contours of positive human health. *Psychological Inquiry*, 9(1) 1–28 and Ryff, C. D., & Singer, B. (2007). Know thyself and become what you are: A eudaimonic approach to psychological well-being. *Journal of Happiness Studies*, 9:13–39.

these ideas with the thinking of Maslow and Rogers is quite striking and lends further credibility to the original *eudaimonic* model.

IT'S NOT EASY

In Aristotle's *Ethics* the word "*ought*" appears quite frequently. Actualization theorists like Aristotle, Maslow, Rogers, and others make no secret of their view that we have an obligation to become all that we are able.

Aristotle's *eudaimonia* derives from the Ancient Greek word *daimon*. Ones' *daimon* is something like ones' unique spirit, ones' individual inner or true self, or the form of what we really are. Norton[13] suggests that we have a destiny to bring together our *daimon* and our actual self by becoming and fulfilling the *daimon's* potentials. "According to self-actualization ethics it is every person's primary responsibility first to discover the *daimon* within him and thereafter to live in accordance with it." Norton notes that although reaching the perfection of our *daimon* is not possible, it is essential that we do our very best to come as close as we can. Even the potato sprout did not give up. To quit is to die. Rogers reminds us that we cannot destroy the urge to grow without destroying the organism. Maslow warns us that if we choose to be less than we are able, unhappiness will follow. Existential philosophers tell us that we must be *authentic*.[14] We must be true to ourselves and take responsibility for our own growth and development no matter what the era and no matter what the external forces working against us are. We must be responsible for our own lives, we must listen to and follow our *daimon*. To fail is to fail at life.

13 Norton, D. L. (1976). *Personal destinies: A philosophy of ethical individualism.* New Jersey: Princeton University Press.

14 Kaufmann, W. (Ed.) (1961). *Existentialism: From Dostoevsky to Sartre.* Cleveland, OH:Meridian Books.

In theory, actualizing is required of all of us but in the real world it is no easy task. There are very strong forces out there trying to mold us and fit us into niches not of our choosing. It is well and good that we are what we are, and it is well and good that the world strives to protect itself from our individuality or our unique *daimons.* The struggle between society and the individual is guaranteed for all time. It has been a major concern for countless philosophers and psychologists including Freud who was convinced that as we become more civilized and controlled by social institutions, the less we are able to be true to ourselves.[15]

I would like to briefly note here some agreement with Freud, but also take some exception to his thoughts on the subject. In today's world, even more than in Freud's time, the social forces limiting our individuality are enormously powerful. We have grown a little deaf to the idea of individual *daimons* and the necessity to be ourselves. The successful person of today is usually thought of as one who conforms to the social demands and becomes not what his *daimon* requests, but what his family, community, employer, and so on require. Given the variety of unique *daimons* among us, it is unlikely that we are all meant to be lawyers, computer experts, public speakers, or good students. But, unfortunately, our educational systems and many of our social institutions often fail to recognize talents outside the ones they esteem. IQ is not everything, or at least it should not be everything. Howard Gardner[16] has argued very persuasively for a more inclusive definition of intelligence that contains at least eight different forms rather than the two (verbal and quantitative) evaluated by traditional IQ measures. Gardner proposes that each of us possess a unique combination of logical-mathematical intelligence, linguistic intelligence, spatial intelligence (ability to manipulate mental images),

[15] Freud, S. (1961/1930). *Civilization and its discontents.* New York: W. W. Norton & Co. Inc.

[16] Gardner, H. (1993). *Multiple intelligences: The theory in practice.* New York: Basic Books.

musical intelligence, kinesthetic intelligence (bodily-movement), interpersonal intelligence (ability to read and relate to other people), intrapersonal intelligence (ability to read and understand ones own feelings and motives) and naturalist intelligence, (the ability to attend to and understand features of the environment).

Gardner's list of intellectual abilities may prove to be far from exhaustive. He has considered a "spiritual intelligence" as well. Others, like Daniel Goleman,[17] have directed our attention to something called *emotional intelligence.* Goleman notes:

> Much evidence testifies that people who are emotionally adept – who know and manage their own feelings well, and who read and deal effectively with other people's feelings-are at an advantage in any domain of life, whether romance and intimate relationships or picking up the unspoken rules that govern success in organizational politics. People with well-developed emotional skills are also more likely to be content and effective in their lives, mastering the habits of mind that foster their own productivity: people who cannot marshal some control over their emotional life fight inner battles that sabotage their ability for focused work and clear thought.

We will return to Goleman's emotional intelligence in a later chapter but the point I'm trying to make here is that our potentials are many. And given that each potential can assume many different levels, the combinations they create are probably infinite, making each of us a unique person. I lament that in our time so few talents and possibilities are valued. It seems as though the world would love us all to be book smart, interpersonally able, and obedient. The fact that today only a few of us with high ability levels in certain areas are rising to the top while most are slowly sliding downward, speaks volumes about our emphasis on some potentials to the neglect of others. We need doctors and lawyers and computer experts sure, but we need

[17] Goleman, D. (1995). *Emotional intelligence.* New York: Bantam Books, p. 36.

artists, teachers, nurturing parents, and courageous warriors, too. We need the gadfly and the critic to keep us awake and open to alternatives. There is good reason to value the many possibilities within each of us.

To "be what you is" isn't easy. It's hard to discover potentials and it's harder still to be guided by them. Unconditional positive regard is in short supply but we are urged to do all that we can to become ourselves. We *ought* to do the best we can. We are obligated to give it our best shot. We need to work as hard at living well as we do at earning a living.

5

Finding Potentials

Know thyself.
Socrates (469–399 B.C.)

Aristotle's idea that living things have potentials in need of actualization is the bedrock of Humanistic psychology as well as the basis of the U.S. Army commercial that urges young people to "be all that you can be." The notion of individual fulfillment, however, has seen its ups and downs.

Following the Classical Greek period of Socrates, Plato, and Aristotle, Athens was conquered by the Roman Empire. Constantine, one of the early Roman emperors, accepted Christianity as did most of the later emperors and within a few hundred years almost the whole of Europe was ruled by the Church. For most of Christianity's first 1,000 years, the idea of fulfillment had nothing to do with individuality or human potentials but rather eternal salvation; that is, happiness is not of this world but lies only in the next.

Psychologist Roy Baumeister[1] reviewed the history of the concept of self and found that with the exception of a just a few writers, interest in human uniqueness was absent during the Middle Ages and did not reappear until the Romantic era of the late eighteenth and early nineteenth centuries. Baumeister notes, "The Romantic era is perhaps best known for its quests to replace Christian salvation

[1] Baumeister, R. (1987). How the self became a problem: A psychological review of historical research. *Journal of Personality and Social Psychology*, 52, 163–176.

with viable, secular images of human fulfillment in life on earth." Elsewhere he says, "The Romantic era is well known for its experimentation with new ideas of human fulfillment. These focused on work, especially in art and literature, and subjective passion, especially love. In addition, a vague but important interest in the cultivation of ones inner qualities emerged."[2] Thus, individuality, selfhood, and human potentials, although ancient ideas, are actually relatively new to us and only poorly understood even today.

Psychologist Mihaly Csikszentmihalyi (pronounced "cheeks sent me high") writes in his book *The Evolving Self*[3] that as our human brain increased in complexity, the ability to integrate and synthesize information also developed. Just as our perception synthesizes the trees and other vegetation on the hillside to form what we call the forest, we unify the various aspects of our own being and call it our "self." Csikszentmihalyi suggests then that the self is a creation where selected aspects are integrated and unified into a meaningful whole. Because the self is a creation of our own making, it can take a variety of forms and need not necessarily mirror what is.

For hundreds of years, however, there was little interest in what we now call the "self." Freud's psychoanalytic theory was an early attempt to resurrect the inner person long oppressed during the Middle Ages and then again in the Victorian era with its emphasis on appearances and social acceptability.

Erik Erikson, a disciple of Freud, offered a revision of Freud's psychosexual stages of development. Where Freud had emphasized the importance of sexual development, Erikson stressed the importance of social relationships and extended the developmental stages beyond puberty, where Freud had left them, into the far reaches of

[2] Baumeister, R. (1986). *Identity: Cultural change and the struggle for self.* New York: Oxford University Press, p. 60.

[3] Csikszentmihalyi, M. (1993). *The evolving self: A psychology for the third millennium.* New York: HarperCollins Publishers.

adulthood.[4] One of his most well-known stages describes adolescent development and is known as the stage of *identity versus role confusion*. It was Erikson's view that young adults strive to discover and create a sense of "self" or "me" that eventually becomes a self-definition. The self is characterized mainly by a set of goals, values, and beliefs to which the person becomes committed. The process of commitment occurs over time and while adolescence is crucial to identity formation, we continue to develop over our lifetimes. Typically, most identity confusion is resolved as the adolescent gradually finds an occupational, political, and moral self, as well as other selves such as a gender and spiritual self.

Eriksen's stage of identity development is not exactly the same as the discovery of potentials, but the two processes have a lot in common. Identity cannot be established independent of built-in, native dispositions. The athlete, scholar, and rock musician must begin with something inherent and given. But genetic material either flowers or is frustrated depending upon the environment in which it finds itself. As with the proverbial acorn, the possibilities within the self are partly at the mercy of the world. Potentials and world must work together if we are to become ourselves.

Marcia[5] observes the various "statuses" that identification can assume depending upon the support of the social environment. Some young people experience a *moratorium*. For one reason or another, these individuals can't seem to find their potentials or the support needed for their expression. Lacking an identity, they have difficulty separating from parents and establishing a sense of selfhood. Their identity crisis is ongoing but they continue the search. A second status of identification is *foreclosure*. Foreclosures have been unable to work through their own identities and merge their unique recipe of

[4] Erikson, E. H. (1964). *Insight and responsibility* New York: W.W. Norton & C. Inc.

[5] Marcia, J. E. (1980). Identity in adolescence. In J. Adelson (Ed.) *Handbook of adolescent psychology*. New York: Wiley.

potentials with the demands of the social environment. Instead they have taken on the values, ideas, and beliefs of family and authority. These people tend to be quite rigid and conforming to traditional ways, accepting and defending them as their own. The third of Marcia's statuses is *diffusion*. Some people have been unable to synthesize their potentials with the social forces of their world and have therefore put off any integration of the two. They make no commitments to either self or world but remain undefined. These people tend to suffer more than the others, drifting without devotion to anything. They therefore tend to be rather poor at establishing and maintaining social bonds and lack any central core of individuality. Finally, Marcia points to those who are successful in solving their identity crisis, *achieving* or at least on their way to a meaningful identity. These people are the best adjusted, happiest, and most psychologically secure. They have been able to integrate potentials with the demands of the world to establish a unique identity and a sense of selfhood.

Csikszentmihalyi, together with his colleagues,[6] studied the psychological growth of a group of adolescents they called "talented teenagers." Their findings cast some light on the general problem of the discovery and development of human potentials.

Csikszentmihalyi's teenagers were selected because of their extraordinary talents in one or more of several fields or domains of study: mathematics, science, music, art, and athletics. The investigators assumed that the origins of talent lay in genetic determinants.

> "Some of us are born with genes that will make us grow tall; others are destined to stay relatively short. Some children can

[6] Csikszentmihalyi, M., Rathunde, K., & Whalen, S. & Wong, M. (1993). *Talented teenagers: The roots of success and failure* (pp. 22–23). London: Cambridge University Press. Also see Waterman, A. S. (Ed.) (1985) *Identity in adolescence: Processes and contents. New Directions for Child Development*, #30, San Francisco: Jossey-Bass Inc., and Kroger, J. (2004). *Identity in adolescence: The balance between self and other.* New York: Routledge, Taylor & Francis Group.

> acquire perfect pitch without much effort; others never learn to carry a tune. Some are endowed from early childhood with superior spatial visualization; others are obviously athletic or double jointed or gifted with particularly fast reflexes. How such gifts are distributed remains a mystery. Inevitably they must originate with the genes of some ancestor, distant or recent.... The great diversity of **potentials** is part of the evolutionary strategy of the human race" (pp. 22–23).

Csikszentmihalyi and colleagues also note that talent doesn't come full blown in an all-or-nothing form but rather *develops*: "Children are talented only in the sense of future potential; to fulfill that potential, they will have to learn to perform to state-of-the-art standards."

Fulfilling their extraordinary potentials was not up to the teenagers alone. Help from several sources was needed. First, their families were very important. The young people who went on to discover and develop their potentials had support from family members who offered encouragement, consistency, and the time required for sustained attention to their field. Parents can also help by allowing their children to experience failure on occasion so that they discover where their talents lie. Further, the study found that teachers had an important impact on their students' development. "What most intrigues students about these teachers is their enthusiasm for subjects that seemed boring and purposeless in other teachers' classes." Good teachers not only showed excitement for their field but also challenged and encouraged the special teenagers to excel in their chosen domains. They didn't just transmit information, they modeled interest and commitment to their field. Effective teachers were remembered by students for being genuinely interested and supportive of their talents.

Perhaps most importantly, Csikszentmihalyi and colleagues found that talented teenagers *enjoyed* pursuing their interests. Intrinsic motivation – the simple joy of working on a task or project – was a major factor in the youths' development. Such enjoyment has been the major concern of Csikszentmihalyi's work for many years.[7] There is a special form of intrinsic motivation that he calls *flow*. Flow happens when we become engrossed in what we are doing and has the effect of not only sustaining the activity and creating pleasure, but also develops the mind. Let's look at the role of flow in the pursuit of fulfillment.

Have you ever been so engrossed in an activity that you lost your sense of time and space, and even your sense of self? It might have happened while you were playing a computer game, reading a book, or baking a cake; the specific activity is not what's important. Rather, it is the state of consciousness that accompanies the activity. On those rare occasions when the task, problem, or activity is perfectly matched to your expertise, when you are moving toward accomplishing what you set out to do, and when you feel in control of the situation, a feeling of exhilaration and excitement comes over you and displaces the sense of self that is usually experienced. Csikszentmihalyi calls such a feeling *optimal experience or flow*. Flow never happens to us when we are passive. It can't happen while we watch TV or stare off into space. Rather, the mind and body have to be engaged, active, working toward a goal, and making progress. Flow takes effort and creativity. It requires a deep level of attention and concentration.

Flow or optimal experience may very well happen when we are in pursuit of fulfillment, working toward developing our artistic, athletic, nurturing, or mathematical potentials. Intrinsic motivation comes from the joy of doing what we like to do. We want to do it, like to do it, and find doing it enjoyable. Flow is a kind of intrinsic motivation but is even more profound. Flow requires a certain level of complexity in the brain and as it occurs, it adds further to that

[7] Csikszentmihalyi, M. (1990). *Flow: The psychology of optimal experience*. New York: Harper/Collins Publishers. The quotation about meaning can be found on p. 216.

complexity. Flow means we are doing something right. Flow means growth, development, and fulfillment in progress.

There is another idea that Csikszentmihalyi has given to us that deserves a brief mention here. He observes that flow requires a certain level of psychological development and that as flow becomes more common and more a part of life, the various parts of that life come together to form a unity. Whenever flow occurs there is a purpose involved, and when a purpose pervades ones' life then there is unity and meaningfulness. "Creating meaning involves bringing order to the contents of the mind by integrating one's actions into a unified flow experience." As Csikszentmihalyi tells us, a bunch of unrelated flow experiences is not enough for a good life. However, if one finds a singular purpose, such as "Do unto others as you would have done to you," or "My purpose in life is to be the finest athlete I can," then all actions are related and all actions are meaningful. Flow characterizes the life as a whole.

But our main point here is that one of the ways that Csikszentmihalyi's talented teenagers discovered their potentials and worked at developing them was by experiencing flow. When they felt that sense of exhilaration and wonderful pure engagement they were on their way. While they were temporarily losing a sense of self they were building a more complex but more unified self. They were finding potentials and developing them and were actualizing possibilities.

Psychologist Alan Waterman with his colleagues[8] suggest that identity development proceeds most successfully when we engage in activities that reveal our potentials. That is when there is (1) a balance between our abilities and the challenges of the task, (2) when we feel that we are moving toward goals and developing potentials,

[8] Waterman, A. S., Schwartz, S. J., & Conti, R. (2008). The implications of two conceptions of happiness (hedonic enjoyment and eudaimonia) for the understanding of intrinsic motivation. *Journal of Happiness Studies*, 9, 41–79.

(3) when we are willing to invest a lot of effort, and (4) when we think the activity is important. They found that when people participated in such activities they felt alive, involved, fulfilled, and true to themselves. Waterman called these feelings "personal expressiveness" or the *experience of eudaimonia.*

It is easy to be fooled into thinking that "identity" is something that goes on mainly when we are young like Csikszentmihalyi's teenagers. However, a little reflection tells us that self-concept and self-knowledge are truly ever-changing processes. All of us to some degree and with more or less success continuously strive for a clearer picture of ourselves. Parents, family, friends, and even strangers offer us hints whether we want them or not. Establishing a sense of "me" requires input from many sources in the world as well as a heavy dose of introspection. Introspection or self-observation is difficult and many of us avoid it like the plague. But knowing thyself has infinite value. In her book on character, virtue, and vice, McKinnon[9] observers "Correct self-perception and other-perception will be requisites of a good life. One must understand what kind of being one is as well as conceive of the particular being that one wants to become, and one must recognize that other persons are also beings of the relevant sort, engaged in similar kinds of pursuit."

What we know of ourselves dictates most of our actions – the career we pursue, the mate we select, the friends we keep, and the politics we practice. We are not just bundles of habits and disconnected actions. Our lives have cohesiveness and meaning. There is a central core to us. Our creation of self governs even as it undergoes continuous adjustment and restructuring.

Restructuring or reconfiguring the self has been the goal of several forms of psychotherapy and counseling. Psychotherapy is no

[9] McKinnon, C. (1999). *Character, virtue theories, and the vices.* Ontario, Canada: Broadview Press, p. 51.

longer restricted to correcting deficiencies[10] but is often devoted to personal growth and the development of well-being.

Carl Rogers' client-centered therapy[11] nicely demonstrates the operation of self and the conditions necessary for its healthy development. Rogers' therapy aims at strengthening the client's self-concept because that is where behavior and emotion begin. When we reconfigure the sense of self, everything changes.

Rogers assumes that clients come to him with the will to improve their lives. The *actualizing tendency* provides the motivation to grow. To this end Rogers offers the client understanding, empathy, and a safe and supportive setting. As the client explores his or her true feelings, desires, and *potentials*, restructuring occurs and self-confidence grows stronger. Therapy is not only for the disabled and suffering; it can provide a means of growth and fulfillment. But such therapy requires hard work in the area of self-exploration and an honest assessment of potentials. Thus, counseling and psychotherapy can be other routes to discovery of potentials. But there are still other avenues as well.

Psychologist John Clausen[12] found adult men and women sometimes experience life-changing views of themselves, which he called "turning points." Elaine Wethington[13] has studied such turning points and found that they come in many forms, both positive and negative. Among the most powerful turning points are health problems, work and career events, parenthood, marriage, sexual relationships, and the illness and death of others. Wethington found that

10 Mearns, D., & Thorne, B. (2000). *Person-centered therapy today: New frontiers in theory and practice.* Thousand Oaks, CA: Sage Publications.

11 Rogers, C. (1961). *On becoming a person: A therapist's view of psychotherapy.* Boston: Houghton Mifflin.

12 Clausen, J. A. *American lives: Looking back at the children of the Great Depression.* (1993). New York: The Free Press.

13 Wethington, E. (2003). Turning points as opportunities for psychological growth. In C. L. M. Keys, & J. Haidt (Eds.), *Flourishing: Positive psychology and the life well-lived.* Washington, D.C.: American Psychological Association.

"perceptions of growth and strength are often born out of suffering and setbacks, as well as accomplishments and achievements." Psychologist Jack Bauer and colleagues[14] suggest that redemption of the self has always been part of the American character. So the self need not be fixed at any age but rather can undergo even dramatic changes well into adulthood. And "suffering and setbacks" can and often do contribute to growth.

Although ideas like self-image, self-confidence, and self-concept seem as if they have been around forever, they are relatively recent ideas in the history of our species. The discovery of self and an understanding of the conditions necessary for its healthy development have only just begun. While Aristotle tells us that knowledge of potentials is essential to a good life, he has little to say about how this knowledge might be acquired. Contemporary psychology has made important contributions to this area but clearly there is more to be done. To "know thyself" is not as easy as Socrates made it seem.

[14] Bauer, J. J., McAdams, D. P., & Pals, J. (2008). Narrative identity and eudaimonic well-being. *Journal of Happiness Studies*, *9*, 81–104.

6

The Things We Need to Be Happy: Goods, Intrinsic Motivation, and The Golden Mean

> if any one gives too great a power to anything, too large a sail to a vessel, too much food to the body, too much authority to the mind, and does not observe the mean, everything is overthrown.
>
> Plato, *Laws III*, 691

Nathaniel Hawthorne claimed that happiness comes to us like a butterfly, alighting on our shoulder when we least expect it. That's a wonderfully romantic idea but probably wrong. A good life usually comes slowly, over time, and requires effort. Benjamin Franklin said "The Declaration only guarantees the American people the right to pursue happiness. You have to catch it yourself."

Happiness requires the satisfaction of many needs. Remember Maslow's hierarchy and that, depending upon our place along the hierarchy, we desire and seek the things that we need. For the hungry it is nourishment, for the homeless it is security, and for the lonely it is friendship.

According to Aristotle, the things we seek are "goods." Goods may differ among us – what is a good for one person may be of little interest to another if they are at different places along the hierarchy of needs. Poetry, science, and philosophy are of little importance to the hungry and the fearful. Goods are defined relative to needs and needs lower on the hierarchy must come first.

Aristotle was a *teleologist*; he believed that we are goal seeking and that all behaviors have an aim, an end, or a purpose. The final end is, of course, fulfillment or happiness, but along the way we need more basic goods like food, friends, and self-confidence. Recall that Aristotle called these and other necessities *real goods*. He recognized the difference between needs and wants. A new car, a piece of jewelry, an expensive dress may be desirable but they don't fulfill any human need. No one needs a mansion. One might need a car to get to work and to perform the tasks of everyday living but no one needs a new Hummer. You may want an expensive vacation but you don't need it. Which of Maslow's needs might be satisfied by an expensive car or a hillside villa?

Aristotle called the things we want but don't really need *apparent goods*. Apparent goods usually give us pleasure but don't help us to grow. They don't change us in any significant way and add little of importance to our lives.

There is nothing wrong with apparent goods. I like old watches, my friend collects expensive bicycles, and a neighbor collects old tools. You might like antiques or recipes or movies. Good for all of us. Apparent goods are fun, make us feel good, and give us a boost every now and then. But we should recognize them for what they are – apparent goods – they will never make us happy.

There are a lot of people who do not understand the distinction between real and apparent goods. Millions confuse the two, focusing on the pleasure that accompanies both. Pleasure is nice and there is nothing wrong with it, but it can come from good choices or poor ones. Some spend their whole lives chasing after expensive cars, diamonds, big houses, power, and recognition. But momentary pleasures do not add up to happiness. A good life comes from growing, actualizing, and fulfilling possibilities, and these require real, not apparent goods.

Edward Deci,[1] a prominent psychologist who has studied motivation for many years, noted long ago that we sometimes fall out

[1] Deci, E. (1980). *The psychology of self-determination*. Lexington, MA: Lexington Books.

of touch with our needs and our genuine motives. As Carl Rogers described it, we fail to do adequate *organsmic listening.* Deci suggests that when we fail to listen to our authentic needs, we often invent substitutes for them. We have all heard about people who substitute food for love. And what about the fanatical collector who must have every Beanie Baby, doll, or every pocket knife? There are those who pursue power or extreme wealth and neglect their families and friends and even their own health. Deci would say these people have developed substitute motives while authentic ones remain hidden and out of consciousness.

Let me stress again that there is nothing wrong with apparent goods or the pleasures that derive from them, but pleasure comes from more than "getting." As we saw in the previous chapter, athletes enjoy playing sports, artists enjoy painting, and musicians love making music. Writing is hard work but pleasurable to the poet, and although parenting is hard work it is pleasurable to the devoted mother or father. Pleasure in the pursuit of real goods often comes not so much from "getting" but from "doing." Doing what is good for the body and soul is pleasurable. The active pursuit of need fulfillment, as long as there is some progress, is enjoyable in its own right and may even be accompanied by *flow.* As a graduate student I learned to truly enjoy studying, loosing track of time, and sometimes forgetting to eat. Repairing watches can be fun and so can gardening. Cooking can be satisfying even without the eating that usually follows. The pursuit can be just as gratifying as reaching the goal. As the saying goes, "it's not the destination, it's the journey." Joy comes with meaningful pursuit! Ask any mountain climber.

INTRINSIC MOTIVATION

Aristotle notes that people on their way to a good life enjoy the way they live: "pleasure for each individual consists of what he is said to be a lover of – horses for horse lovers and plays for theater lovers.

In the same way justice is pleasant for the man who loves justice." These people enjoy living as they do and have little need for apparent goods. "Their life has no extra need of pleasure as a kind of wrapper; it contains pleasure in itself." I think what Aristotle is saying here is that striving for real goods is pleasant in itself. Whether he or she wins or loses, a true athlete enjoys playing the game.

This idea is very similar to what contemporary psychology calls *intrinsic motivation*.[2] Intrinsic motivation comes from the inherent tendency to fulfill needs. Climbing mountains, working crossword puzzles, practicing the piano, or chatting with a friend are intrinsically motivated. No external rewards need be involved. If winning a trophy was all that was in it for team members there would be few players. Exercise is fun when we choose it but painful when we do not. Learning is best when motivated by interest and curiosity. Art and science are best when driven by passion, curiosity, and love. A composer might take money from a sponsor but without the passion to create something of beauty, the music will never be noteworthy. Those actions that stem from needs come from within. Truly talented performers, artists, and scientists pursue their craft regardless of outside forces or rewards. They do what they do because they love it. The activity itself is the reward.

Extrinsic motivation can be powerful too but it operates differently than intrinsic motivation. Extrinsic rewards are things outside of us that motivate action. A trophy, a piece of jewelry, an A grade on an exam, and a new toy are motivators too, and they can have powerful effects on our actions.

An enormous amount of psychological theory and research has concerned itself with the effects of extrinsic reward or reinforcement.

[2] Deci, E. (1975). *Intrinsic motivation*. New York: Plenum Press. See also Ryan, R. M., & Deci, E. L. (2000). Self-determination theory and the facilitation of intrinsic motivation, social development, and well-being. *American Psychologist*, 55, 68–78 and Deci, E. L., & Ryan, R. M. (1985). *Intrinsic motivation and self-determination in human behavior*. New York: Plenum Press.

At the end of the nineteenth century Edward Thorndike proposed the "law of effect." Reward has the *effect* of strengthening behavior. The law, simply stated, suggests that behaviors followed by extrinsic rewards (like money or candy), will tend to recur. So, if you want your children to clean their rooms or do well in school, reward them for those behaviors. When our children were young, my wife called this tactic bribery and used it very effectively. After a successful trip to the potty chair my two-year-old granddaughter Hannah smiles and says "catchca," which in her lingo means chocolate. She has learned well that when she uses the potty chair she gets a reward. B. F. Skinner, the late leader of the Behavioral Psychology movement, believed the "law of effect" has enormous potential for changing both individual behavior and society.[3] His work has influenced education, business, psychotherapy, and just about every other sector of our culture. The idea is simple: Reward desired behaviors and ignore (don't reward) the undesirable ones. (Notice that Skinner had little confidence in the power of punishment claiming that simply not rewarding is enough to alter behavior.) It is pretty much accepted as gospel in our time. We reward children who do well in school, employees who work well, actions that benefit the environment, and the wayward who reshape their lives. Athletes are rewarded with high salaries and tax breaks go to businesses that cooperate with government. As Skinner claimed, we are at the mercy of rewards. We do what they tell us. Bribery works and everybody, from little kids to the government, knows it.

THE INTERACTION BETWEEN INTRINSIC AND EXTRINSIC REWARDS

There are, then, two motivational forces: the internal needs like those identified by Maslow (physiological needs, safety and security,

[3] Skinner, B. F. (1948). *Walden two.* New York: The Macmillan Co.

etc.) and the external forces (extrinsic rewards, punishments, and threats).

It is easy to imagine that the two forces are additive and work together. That is, being paid to do something you like is better than doing it for love alone. Money plus fun is better that fun alone. Actually, it's not that simple. The relationship between intrinsic and extrinsic motivation is complex, surprising, and sometimes counter-intuitive. It has been studied under several headings but perhaps the one called "*the crowding effect of extrinsic reward*"[4] is most revealing.

Extrinsic rewards can overwhelm and control us even when our real needs or intrinsic motives wish otherwise. How many of us remain in jobs that have become unsatisfying? How many students study for grades instead of trying to satisfy their inherent hunger for knowledge? It is not uncommon for performers to start out with a passion for their art but eventually become slaves to agents and the paying public who control their appearances and choice of performance material and even their very lives. The money rock stars earn becomes the controlling agent and the authentic, intrinsic motive that used to direct their talents now has been overpowered by the rewards of fame and fortune.

There is a huge literature on the detrimental effects of extrinsic rewards on intrinsic motivation and it may be helpful to briefly review it here in order to emphasize the important difference between Aristotle's real and apparent goods.

Back in the 1950s, psychologist Robert White[5] introduced an idea called "*competence motivation.*" White noticed that little kids

[4] Frey, B. S., & Jegen, R. *Motivation crowding theory: A survey of empirical evidence.* (1999). Working Paper No. 26. Working Paper Series ISSN 1424-0459. Institute for Empirical Research in Economics, Universe of Zurich. Available at www.landecon.cam.ac.uk/speer/iewwp026.pdf

[5] White, R. (1959). Motivation reconsidered: The concept of competence. *Psychological Review, 66*, 297–333.

do a lot of things without the introduction of rewards. They climb monkey bars, practice skipping, and walk up and down the stairs a million times just for the fun of it. Similarly, millions play video games, work crossword puzzles, climb mountains, cook, and play basketball. Why? What's the reward? White proposed that extrinsic rewards play no part here, rather it is the feeling of competence, control, and mastery that we experience. We all have a need to be good at what we do and to be effective when we interact with the world. This need explains our actions; extrinsic reward does not.

A few years later, Richard DeCharms[6] elaborated this idea and suggested that we have a need to be in control of our lives. We need to feel as if we choose what we do. As he put it, we need to be the "*locus of causality*" for our actions. When *we* decide what to do we are empowered, feel competent, and experience growth in self-esteem and confidence. On the other hand, when we are forced to do something, we experience weakness and feel like pawns driven by forces beyond our control. The same action with the same outcome may have very different effects. If Jean cleans her room because she is forced, against her will, then she may feel weak and compliant. However, if *she* decides to clean her room then she is the cause of her actions, in control, and feels good about it. Coercion and extrinsic reward have similar effects: Both are outside forces that direct behavior. We need to experience ourselves as causal and as self-determining. Extrinsic reward can take that control away from us.

In recent years psychologists have carried this idea further and studied the relationship between the inside and outside forces that drive us. In countless laboratory experiments, real life situations, and field studies it has been observed that internal needs get *crowded out* by external rewards. Millions of students who once enjoyed learning now do so only to pass tests and get acceptable grades. Their inherent

6 DeCharms, R. (1968). *Personal causation: The internal affective determinants of behavior.* New York: Academic Press.

interest in learning has been *crowded out* by a more powerful external force … grades.

As noted many times here, we have basic physiological, security, and self-esteem needs. When we recognize these needs and are able to fulfill them, we feel strong and competent. When our needs govern our actions and our actions are effective, we thrive. When our needs go unnoticed or unmet and our actions are directed by external forces like rewards, punishments, social demands, and the like, we feel diminished, weak, and out of control. While extrinsic rewards can be powerful determinants of behavior and invaluable when correctly used as in certain instances of behavior modification, they can also be profoundly damaging. This goes against quite a lot of accepted psychological theory, but external forces – be they threats, punishments, social pressures, or money – can be harmful to our well-being.

A dramatic example of the harmful effects of external control was observed years ago by Martin Seligman, now a leader in the Positive Psychology movement.[7] Positive Psychology focuses on well-being, mental health, happiness, and the good life, as opposed to the pathologies that consumed psychology for so long. Before Seligman became involved with well-being he performed experiments on what came to be called "learned helplessness."[8] His experiments with both animals and humans exposed subjects to uncontrollable conditions like electric shock, noise, or unsolvable problems and watched what happened. Seligman likened the effect of these conditions to depression. Depression is associated with passivity, decline in social interaction, inability to learn, and so on. In experiments with dogs that were unable to escape shock, the animals learned to be helpless. Later, when they could easily escape the shock they just laid there

[7] Snyder, C. R., & Lopez, S. J. (Eds.) (2002). *Handbook of positive psychology.* New York: Oxford University Press.

[8] Seligman, M. E. (1975). *Helplessness.* San Francisco: W. H. Freeman and Co.

and accepted it. They even had difficulty learning to walk from the shock side to the safe side of the cage. Seligman working with his colleagues also showed that the effect of uncontrollability was not limited to painful stimuli. When pigeons received grain at random and had no control over the reward, they too experienced motivational deficits and had difficulty learning how to regain control. When college students were paid for working anagram puzzles and then given the opportunity to return to the ones they were unable to solve, they were much less likely to do so than subjects who were not paid. Not only do electric shocks cause loss of control but so do positive rewards like money. When negative or positive extrinsic forces are applied, we tend to let them *crowd out* our intrinsic needs and we then suffer the consequences.

Deci, Koestner, and Ryan[9] reviewed over 100 experiments on the de-motivating effects of extrinsic rewards. They find "clear and consistent" evidence of how tangible rewards like money, candy, and prizes can reduce interest in a task and "this effect showed up with participants ranging from preschool to college, with interesting activities ranging from word games to construction puzzles, and various rewards ranging from dollar bills to marshmallows."

There is an old story about a Jewish store owner in Germany just before World War II. Nazi youth decided to taunt the poor man each morning outside his small shop. After a few frightening days the merchant approached the youths with an offer to pay them for their efforts. This went on for a few days and each morning the boys laughed as they pocketed the money. Soon the forlorn shop keeper again approached the bullies explaining that since his business had been so damaged he would no longer be able to pay them. The boys angrily shouted they were not going to come out each morning and

[9] Deci, E. L., Koestner, R., & Ryan, R. M. (1999) A meta-analytic review of experiments examining the effects of extrinsic rewards on intrinsic motivation. *Psychological Bulletin, 25*, 627–668.

taunt him for nothing! The poor shop keeper knew, before psychological research proved it, that extrinsic reward can reduce intrinsic motivation.

While the diminishing effects of extrinsic reward on intrinsic motivation is well documented, the complexity of the relationship should not be underestimated. Deci, Koestner, and Ryan found that tangible rewards such as money have very different effects than verbal rewards like praise. Praise and positive feedback can actually increase intrinsic motivation by adding to one's sense of mastery and control. The researchers also note the importance of age, because young children seem to interpret rewards as controlling and are therefore more strongly impacted by them. Verbal reward may be perceived as either controlling or confirming of autonomy, depending on how it is delivered. The *crowding out effect* is strong and reliable but also pretty complicated. Extrinsic rewards should be used carefully and in an informed way.

Returning to Aristotle's real and apparent goods, we may conclude that real goods are those things and conditions that satisfy needs. Food, friendship, and competence are real goods. Apparent goods may be pleasurable but do not fulfill any innate human needs. They can be thought of as extrinsic rewards that can indeed be powerful determiners of behavior, even taking over our lives. Psychologists Tim Kasser and Richard Ryan, in an article entitled "A Dark Side of the American Dream"[10] warn us that an emphasis on financial success can actually be harmful. Subjects whose central aspiration was financial success were less well adjusted than those who aspired to self-acceptance, affiliation, and feelings of community. Three studies led them to conclude: "Finally, the data suggest that, relatively speaking, the desire for money does not necessarily bring happiness;

[10] Kasser, T., & Ryan, R. M. (1993). A dark side of the American dream: Correlates of financial success as a central life aspiration. *Journal of Personality and Social Psychology*, 65, 410–422.

instead, too much emphasis on this aspect of the American dream may be an organsmic nightmare."

Working for money, fame, or expensive toys can get the best of us. Consider the millions of Americans who work so hard to pay for the cars, boats, vacations, clothes, and the like that almost always prove a disappointment. The following short story seems to convey the point.

> An American businessman on vacation in Mexico noticed a young fisherman who worked very hard and was extremely good at what he did. Upon returning from a days' work on the ocean the man traded his catch to the owner of the boat and received wages in return. Observing this routine over a couple of days the American tourist approached the young fisherman and asked him why he didn't go into business for himself. The native responded by saying "Why would I want to do that? I would not be able to spend time with my wife and children?"
>
> The businessman quickly replied that if he bought his own boat and reaped the profits from his hard work then he could buy other boats and hire other fisherman and make more money. And, success at the fishing business may bring the opportunity to build his own packing house and then he could export his product all over the world. "Why would I want to do that?" inquired the fisherman.
>
> So that you can spend more time with your wife and children replied the American.

Real goods fulfill needs. Intrinsic motivation directs us toward real goods and as we acquire them we move up the hierarchy toward a good human life and Aristotle's *eudaimonia*.

In fact, Deci and colleagues[11] define *eudaimonia* in terms of intrinsic motivation. They suggest that *eudaimonic living* is present when: (1) we are in pursuit of intrinsic goals and values like growth,

[11] Ryan, R. M., Huta, V., & Deci, E. L. (2008). Living well: A self-determination theory perspective of eudaimonia. *Journal of Happiness Studies*, 9,139–170.

friendship, community, and the like, rather than extrinsic goals like fame and fortune; (2) our actions are under our control rather than driven by outside forces; (3) we are acting with awareness and mindfulness rather than blind habit and automaticity; and (4) we are acting to fulfill basic human needs, like the need for autonomy, competence, and relatedness. When we participate in *eudaimonic* living, we are living well and are happy.

Apparent goods are extrinsic rewards, pleasurable but not fulfilling. In fact they often direct our attention away from real needs. Apparent goods, as extrinsic rewards, can take control of our behavior and misdirect our lives. Ancient philosophy and contemporary psychology agree. Real goods move us toward a good life. Apparent goods may be enjoyable, but can, and often do, mislead us. The fisherman had it right.

THE GOLDEN MEAN

Now that we are familiar with the difference between real and apparent goods, we turn to another dimension of "good" that needs to be addressed. How much of a good is really good?

Food, a safe and comfortable home, and friends are all real goods. But how much food or how many friends or how large a house is good for you? Are those common phrases like "the more the better" and "you can't get too much of a good thing" correct? It doesn't take a genius to realize that you can have too little or too much food. On the one hand you might starve and on the other you could become obese. What about coming into a fortune? What if you won the lottery and fell into millions of dollars? Could you handle it or would you, like most lottery winners, be broke within a few years? Do you have the "know how" and the self discipline to manage a fortune? Would a lot of money really be good for you?

Aristotle understood that most goods are *limited goods* and must be present in a certain amount to be really good. Too little food will impair your health while too much can do the same. Like most things, food is a limited good; what is right for a large adult is obviously wrong for a toddler. There is a different correct amount for you, for me, and for the toddler. The right amount of any limited good is *always relative to the person.* If you think about it, you can apply this idea to almost any of the things we desire and it seems to be true for both real and apparent goods. We all need companionship but if we are surrounded by too many friends and have no time for the areas of our lives that require solitude we will suffer the consequences of too much of a good thing. A student once told me that his father, a successful housing developer, had not known a restful night in twenty years. With so many ongoing projects he was consumed with business matters even in his sleep. Money is a real good and we need it to buy the necessities of life, but it is easy to see that we can have too much as well as too little. How much money is good? It depends on the person. Some will cope with the responsibilities better than others. For some, depending on abilities, interests, values, and so on, a lot of money can be a good thing. For many of us, a fortune might bring misfortune and even misery. How much of a good is good? It depends! It depends upon the person.

As we consider this problem we come face to face with the *relativity of goods.* Aristotle recognized that all human beings need pretty much the same things and Maslow believed his need hierarchy applied to all. In that sense goods are absolute. All humans need goods associated with survival, safety and security, self-esteem, and so on. What is good for you is also good for me. However, it is also true that we can be at different places on the hierarchy of needs and therefore desire and seek different things. What is good is always relative to the person.

Goods are relative in more than one way. Many people in today's world are not terribly interested in developing self-confidence or being truly actualized because they are preoccupied with trying to just survive. This morning's newspaper cites a UNICEF study that claims 640 million of the world's children lack adequate shelter, 500 million children have no access to sanitation, 400 million lack safe water, and 90 million are severely deprived of nutrition. Clearly, self-esteem and self-actualization are not major concerns for these poor children. What is good for you and what is good for them are worlds apart. We are all human and need the same things to live well but these children must first fulfill their basic needs. What is good depends on one's circumstances. Goods are relative to the person. As humans we need the same goods but we may need them at different times and in different amounts. They are absolutely good but also relatively good.

To be happy and live well we must fulfill our human needs and, as we have seen, that is not as simple as it might appear. The butterfly is unlikely to land on our shoulder; it's up to us to catch it. To get what we need in the right amount and at the right time requires good thinking and a few other skills to boot. The Greeks had a name for the complex of skills that is so important to fulfillment of needs; they called it *virtue*. Virtue may be the most important idea in all of Greek thought and especially in Aristotle's *Nichomachean Ethics*. Virtue is the subject of the next chapter.

7

Introduction to Virtue

Consider your origin; you were not born to live like brutes, but to follow virtue and knowledge.

Dante Alighieri, *The Divine Comedy* (ca. 1315)

The Ancient Greeks believed that all living things have soul. "Soul" had little or no religious significance back then; it just came with life, all life. Ants and birds, as well as humans, had it, at least as long as they were alive. It is true, however, that souls differed. Human soul was unique because it could reason. Remember, reason was our *ergon*, our defining human characteristic. Cats and cattle can feed themselves, move around, and they can see and hear; they have life and they have soul but they cannot think. We alone understand that "All men are mortal, Socrates is a man, therefore, Socrates is mortal." Because of our ability to reason we are a little closer to the divine.

But we are far from perfect. We also have a powerful irrational side. The *appetitive* part of our soul that houses desires and emotions is often less than reasonable. Fortunately, and this is very important, *the irrational side of us is able to listen to reason and take its advice.* The irrational in us can be influenced by the rational. Aristotle's *moral virtue* is just that: irrational desires, emotions, and actions coming under the influence of reason.[1]

[1] Elliot Cohen's *What Would Aristotle Do?* (2003, Amherst, NY: Prometheus Books) is a readable little book on Aristotle's use of reason to cope with everyday problems. Robert Arrington's *Western Ethics: An Historical Introduction*

Moral virtue is probably the most important idea in Aristotle's ethical writings. The following passage captures the essence of the *Nicomachean Ethics.*

> If virtue, like nature, requires more accuracy and is better than any art, then it will aim at the mean. I speak of *moral virtue*, since that is concerned with emotions and actions; and excess, deficiency, and the mean occur in these. In feeling fear, confidence, desire, anger, pity and in general pleasure and pain, one can feel too much or too little; and both extremes are wrong. *The mean and the good is feeling at the right time, about the right things in relation to the right people and for the right reason;* and *the mean and the good are the task of virtue. Similarly, in regard to actions there are excess, deficiency, and the mean* [italics added].[2]

We typically use the word "moral" to compare an action or thought to some standard, such as a religious ideal, a universal principle, or perhaps a cultural norm. The word is related to "mores" meaning "ways of living." Moral psychology, as presented by William James in the late nineteenth century, and then later by Humanistic Psychology, was devoted to the study of "how we should live."

"Virtue" comes to us from the Latin *virtus. Virtus* was the Roman translation of the Greek *arête*, which means something like "excellence" and applied to cases like the excellence of a knife for cutting or an eye for seeing. But, "virtue" is now rife with excess meanings acquired during the Middle Ages when it was associated with religious authority. "Virtue" is now a rather messy idea but when combined with the word "moral" it retains its ancient meaning: "excellence in living." The Ancient Greeks equated moral virtue with

(1998, Malden, MA: Blackwell Publishers Inc.) has a brief but excellent summary of Aristotle's *Ethics* and is especially clear on the issue of virtue. A thorough account of virtue can be found in Julia Annas' *The Morality of Happiness* (1993, New York: Oxford University Press).

[2] Aristotle. *Nicomachaen Ethics* Book II, Chapter 6.

happiness and, for the Ancient Greeks, moral virtue was the essence of a good human life.

The previous chapter discussed the importance of the *golden mean* to the acquisition of goods, but for Aristotle the *mean* is even more important to our desires, feelings, and actions. When these are at their best we can acquire what we need to fulfill potentials.

The *golden mean* applies then to our emotions and to our behaviors but, as the quotation above notes, the *mean* considers more than just the amount. Moral virtue demands that reason take into account time, place, and circumstance. A particular action might be appropriate in one setting but not in another. It might be perfectly okay to shout to a friend several seats away at a football game but that same action would usually not be acceptable at a religious service. Similarly, sobbing might be fitting at a funeral, but not at a dinner party. From this point of view no emotion or behavior is prohibited but conditions must always be taken into account.

Let's take the example of anger. The moderation suggested in the *golden mean* does not say that one should never be extremely angry; there may well come a time to be legitimately outraged. "One can feel too much or too little; and both extremes are wrong." But remember, the mean is always relative – relative to the person, to time, to place, and circumstance. For example, if someone assaults your child, an extreme emotion and action may be called for. The *golden mean* does not always require a middle ground or average; it requires correctness – correctness for the time and place, and for people and conditions. Outrage or joy – even violence – may, under certain conditions, be the right action.

There is then no simple rule that can be applied to every emotion or action. No emotion or behavior is absolutely forbidden and no emotion or action is absolutely prescribed. According to Aristotle, the best that we can do is, as my father used to say, "use our heads": reason, think, exercise our *ergon*. Let good thinking evaluate the situation and find the right action for the occasion.

Aristotle says that "ethics," that is, the science of the good life, can never be precise, it can only provide general principles like fairness, friendship, and courage. Within the bounds of these principles, reason must be employed to find the right response for the occasion.

Moral virtue describes the relationship among reason, desire, emotion, and behavior. We will explore the connections among these processes in detail a little later in this chapter, but for now we need only to recognize that thoughts, desires, feelings, and actions are very closely tied, sometimes merging together to form a unity, a meaningful whole. To demonstrate their closeness, let's try a little thought experiment.

Think of or imagine an emotional event from your past. As that scene *flows through your mind* you may find yourself *feeling* the same emotions you experienced on the original occasion. You can once again feel the love, the fear, or the anger that you knew in the first instance. Further, you may be able to sense your *body reacting* as it did the first time; muscles may tighten and the heart may race. Thoughts, feelings, and actions combine creating a unity that can be stored in memory and played again and again.

The term "character" has been largely discarded from contemporary culture but the Ancients gave it a prominent place in their thinking about human behavior. As thoughts, feelings, and actions become linked, they can grow into lasting and relatively permanent structures or dispositions. The Greeks called such dispositions *hexes* (the singular is *hexis*), which translates into something like "habits"; a complex habit to desire, think, feel, and act a certain way. One can develop a habit of being honest, friendly, or brave. Being honest is not just a behavior, it includes thinking honestly, wanting to be honest, and feeling good about being honest, as well as performing honest deeds. Such habits become powerful forces in our everyday lives. They become traits of character.

Christopher Peterson and Martin Seligman[3] have recently reintroduced the concepts of character and virtue to psychology, integrating them with the new field of positive psychology. They have tried to identify sources of wellness and happiness just as psychiatrists and clinical psychologists have identified traits that characterize mental illness. Surveying a vast literature of commonly valued traits, they suggest a set of six universal or core virtues with their more specific subordinate character strengths. For example, the virtue of courage refers to one's capacity to endure discomfort for a worthy cause but can be expressed by several character strengths like persistence, bravery, or integrity. The virtues they identify are very like the ones proposed by Aristotle almost 2,500 years ago. A special issue of the *Journal of Happiness Studies*[4] was published shortly after the Peterson and Seligman book, furthering interest in Aristotle's ideas.

We all know of people who have developed poor character traits, people who fail to integrate good reasoning with their feelings and actions and thus put their well-being in jeopardy on a regular basis. They lack the dispositions required to live well. We also know of others who consistently moderate desires, feelings, and actions with good thinking. These people are able to act in adaptive and effective ways, thereby enhancing their own lives and the lives of those around them as well.

To summarize the preceding, moral virtue is the fusion of reason, desire, feeling, and behavior. When these processes merge together by frequent "association," they create a lasting structure which Aristotle called a *hexis* or habit. We come to be habitually fair or selfish, habitually friendly or unfriendly, and habitually brave or cowardly. Our

3 Peterson, C., & Seligman, M. E. P. (2004). *Character strengths and virtues: A handbook and classification*. Oxford: Oxford University Press. Also see Seligman (2002). Authentic happiness. New York: Free Press, for a very readable discussion of character and core virtues in the context of positive psychology.

4 The *Journal of Happiness Studies* (2006). Vol. 7. Springer.

lives eventually develop a consistency, a pattern, a configuration of *hexes.* Moral virtue can take an adaptive form or it can allow the irrational parts of us to have the upper hand. Moral virtue is at the center of human life. Whether we are guided by sound reason and effective desires, feelings and action, or by poor thinking that allows the irrational in us to dominate, moral virtue pretty much decides the quality of our lives.

Aristotle also identified another kind of virtue. *Intellectual virtue* is concerned with understanding basic principles and truths, and the unchanging laws of the universe. Intellectual virtue is very cognitive, involving pure thought, and is less directly concerned with everyday matters that are the focus of moral virtue. However, Aristotle identifies a part of intellectual virtue called *practical wisdom* (*phronesis* in Greek and *Prudencia* or prudence in Latin) that is very important to everyday living.

Practical wisdom enables us to understand what is good and what is bad for us as individuals and as members of a community. It is "the quality of mind concerned with things just and noble and good for man."[5] It understands the principles by which we should live. But practical wisdom is also responsible for analyzing specific situations to calculate how its principles should be applied. In other words, practical wisdom knows what to do and is able to figure out the best way to do it under the circumstances. *Practical wisdom* is an *intellectual virtue*; it is part of our rational soul. While keeping long-term goals related to fulfillment in focus, it is also responsible for taking into account the many factors that define each new situation. *Practical wisdom* deliberates and chooses the best response for the occasion. *Practical wisdom* is a crucial link between the most rational part of the soul and the *moral virtues* that are complexes of reason, irrational desires, and

[5] Aristotle. *Nichomachean Ethics* Book VI, Chapter 12.

feelings.[6] *Practical wisdom* is an intellectual virtue but importantly connected to moral virtue. It operates well at the level of general principles, knowing what is "just and noble," and also at the situational level. It is both theoretical and applied.

Because *practical wisdom* is charged with analyzing circumstances and judging which features are most important, adequate life experience is essential. That is one reason why Aristotle does not expect young people to be truly virtuous. As we will see, virtue must gradually develop. As basic principles like honesty, generosity, or friendship come into focus and the features of situations become identifiable, the child gradually takes control of his or her behavior. Practical wisdom slowly develops and slowly contributes to moral virtue.

In summary, human "soul" has a rational and an irrational side. Moral virtue occurs when reason habitually moderates desire, feeling, and action, bringing the rational and irrational together to find the *golden mean*. *Practical wisdom* is the part of *intellectual virtue* that understands principle and long-term goals while also considering immediate circumstances. *Practical wisdom* is central to moral virtue, taking into account circumstances and using reason to guide action toward constructive ends.

In the next chapter we shall review some of the major moral virtues that Aristotle thought were essential to happiness.

[6] Vallerand, R. J., Blanchard, C., Mageau, G. A., Koestner, R., Ratelle, C., Leonard, M., Gagne, M., & Marsolais, J. (2003) Les Passions de l'Ame: On Obsessive and Harmonious Passion. *Journal of Personality and Social Psychology*, 85, 756–767. Vallerand and colleagues distinguish two kinds of passions or desire to engage in activity. Obsessive passion lacks rational control and demands expression regardless of circumstances and outcome, while harmonious passion takes into account the conditions and usually results in positive affect . For example, they found *obsessively motivated* cyclists in Montreal, Canada, usually cycled even in the severe winters of the region but the equally devoted *harmoniously motivated* usually did not. Vallerand's idea of harmonious passion seems to exemplify Aristotle's notion of *practical wisdom* and its moderating effects on desire.

8

Some of the More Important Moral Virtues

> There is but one law for all, namely, that law which governs all law, the law of our Creator, the law of humanity, justice, equity – the law of nature, and of nations.
>
> Edmund Burke, On the Impeachment of Warren Hastings, 1794[1]

Practical wisdom is an intellectual virtue and part of the rational soul. Ideally, it thinks well as it guides desire, emotion, and behavior according to principle and circumstance. *Practical wisdom* grasps principles like fairness, courage, and friendship, and deliberates about the wisest action for the particular circumstances. It can lead us wisely toward the real goods necessary for fulfillment, or it can mislead us by foolish reasoning. *Practical wisdom* is a fundamental virtue, the bedrock of all the moral virtues and clearly indispensable to a good life.

The *moral virtues* to be discussed in this chapter are different from *practical wisdom* because they are only slightly rational and can be irrational at times. *Moral virtues*, you will recall, are really irrational emotions and their correlated actions, under the sway of prudence or *practical wisdom*, however gifted or feeble that may be. Moral virtues are *hexes*, habitual ways of responding that are developed over a lifetime. They are in a sense automatic, as the term "habit" would imply, but at the same time they are semi-conscious and semi-cognitively

[1] Epigraph may be found at http://www.notable-uotes.com/b/burke_edmund.html

directed by the intelligence of *practical wisdom*. The *moral virtues* determine the way we live, for better or for worse.

It should be added that virtue is not a guarantee of *eudaimonia*. Aristotle clearly recognizes that chance and luck play a role in our lives. An illness, a tragic accident, the horror of war can fall upon us despite the presence of virtue. Given that we can't do very much about it except acknowledge and be open to fates' power, there isn't a whole lot to say about the connection between luck and happiness, so we will leave it that.

If we are fortunate enough to develop sound *moral virtues*, our lives will probably be much easier. We are more likely to be effective persons, accomplishing our goals and moving toward being all that we might. Highly developed *moral virtues* are essential to attaining the real goods we need for fulfillment. The *moral virtues* we now discuss are the means to the end we all seek – happiness.

TEMPERANCE

Temperance is another of those old-fashioned terms that have gathered excess meaning over the centuries. The Ancient Greeks used it to refer to the moderation of pleasure. Keeping in mind that *moral virtues* are a mix of reason and emotion, it is the emotion of pleasure that we are talking about here.

Yes, there is a correct amount of pleasure for each occasion. Too much or too little are both discouraged. Both indulgence and abstinence miss the mark. The *golden mean* is relevant again. Pleasure should be pursued in moderation, taking into account all that Aristotle means by "moderation": time, place, people, and circumstances in general. If we are unable to delay our pleasures and if we make pleasure our primary purpose we are bound to get into trouble. As I will try to explain, temperance is essential to success in all areas of life – in love, in friendship, in business, in the arts, and in all the rest, too; moderation of pleasure is a must.

Our culture is saturated with the notion that a good life is filled with pleasure. Most current psychological research uses "positive affect" or pleasure, or evaluations of pleasures to describe happiness.[2] Educators strive to make learning "fun." Recreational drug and alcohol use is widespread. The media are often used to escape the more unpleasant realities of life, as television, videos, and music stores provide quick fixes for momentary pleasure. Drugs, sex, and thrill seeking seem to have many of us in their grasps. It is as if we cannot get too much of a good thing, pleasure.

"Temperance is the moderation which allows us to be masters of our pleasures instead of becoming their slaves." Have sympathy for those addicted, actually or only nearly, to drugs, sex, thrills, working out, collecting, or eating, to name just a few. They have become slaves to pleasure. It was said of Alexander the Great, conqueror of the world, and a student of Aristotle, that "His body was his servant." That is, Alexander, despite his shortcomings, was not at the mercy of his emotions, but rather, in the tradition of Aristotle, guided by reason (some of the time!).

Can there really be too much pleasure in a life? Not if you believe that pleasure is what truly matters. If you think of pleasure as the first and final good, then temperance makes no sense at all. But if you believe, as I do, that pleasure can be a poor correlate of fulfillment, sometimes accompanying real goods and sometimes not, then the unrelenting quest for fun, thrills, and pleasure is badly flawed.

[2] Diener, E. (2000). Subjective well-being. *American Psychologist*, 55, 34–43. See also Nettle, D. (2005) *Happiness: The science behind your smile*. New York: Oxford University Press, and Kashdan, T. B., Biswas-Diener, R., & King, L. A. (in press) Reconsidering happiness: The costs of distinguishing between hedoncis and eudaimonia. *Journal of Positive Psychology*, as well as Waterman, A. S., Schwartz, S. J., & Conti, R. (2006) The Implications of two conceptions of happiness (hedonic enjoyment and eudaimonia) for the understanding of intrinsic motivation. *Journal of Happiness Studies*, 9, 41–79. All discuss the implications of more than one kind of happiness raising some very provocative and important questions.

The better goal, in Aristotle's eyes, is not just feeling pleasure but moving ahead as a person. Surely we all understand that every pleasure should not be sought after. So often it is our ability to put aside pleasure, at least temporarily, to reach a higher goal, that leads to success.

The search for pleasure might be thought of as an art. We can master the art of pleasure seeking or we can be victimized by its cheaper and more outrages forms. Popular culture would have us addicted to its offerings of sex, violence, and cheap thrills so available in the media. But other forms of pleasure are more worthy. The pleasures of friendship, love, accomplishment, art, and growth in general can be unequalled. How can the rush from a violent film compare to the joy inherent in falling in love or reading a life-altering book, or establishing a true and lasting friendship? We ought to choose our pleasures carefully and become their master. It is not only a matter of how much pleasure; once again we must see the importance of circumstance. There are times to enjoy the pleasures of life and there are times to pass them by. The trick is to be prudent; choose your pleasures wisely according to time, place, and circumstance. Temperance will, in the long run, serve you well. It is likely to guide you past the apparent goods to the real ones, to those that matter.

COURAGE

Courage is another important *moral virtue*. Courage is to pain as temperance is to pleasure. There is an appropriate amount of discomfort for every situation. At one extreme are the cowardly who retreat at the slightest hint of pain. These individuals don't like to be challenged or confronted with adversity of any kind, but rather seek safe and comfortable routes to modest goals. We are all familiar with those who "play it safe" and do their best to avoid any form of discomfort. On the other hand, there are daredevils who seem to relish danger. These people may put their lives in jeopardy on a regular basis, seeming to enjoy the possibility of disaster. We might include those who scale the walls of high buildings for the fun of it or those who jump motorcycles over a row of busses.

In the days of Ancient Greece, courage was greatly but not exclusively concerned with bravery on the battlefield. But bravery can also apply to an infinite range of everyday situations. The student who sticks with the difficult class is being courageous. The mother who sacrifices so much for the welfare of her family is being courageous. The athlete who struggles to stay in good physical condition and who endures the pain inherent in his sport is courageous. The man who toils at a painful job for the sake of his family is being courageous. The examples are infinite.

But, according to the *golden mean*, there is a right amount of suffering for each occasion. Clearly, there are cowards who can't handle even a small amount of pain and discomfort. They complain, they quit, they fall apart at the first sign of distress. And, there are those that don't know when to quit. An abusive boss or class bully should be tolerated only to a point. It is unwise to endure any and all abuse, just as it is unwise to run away from even the smallest unpleasantness.

The person with well-developed moral virtue will know how much is too much, when to walk away, and when to endure. There is a correct amount of courage for each person for each occasion. For one mistreated employee, the correct thing to do may be to stay on the job until the supervisor gets fired for incompetence. For another employee it may be the right time to change careers. There is a kind of relativism here. When to leave is different for each victim. On the other hand, there is a form of absolutism, too. There is a correct time for each to leave. There is an amount of abuse that will push each over the line and cause a separation. One may be able to stick it out and make it work while the other may be better off leaving. The difficulty is in knowing. *Practical wisdom* must deliberate, choose, and advise the moral virtue of courage.

Some will be better than others at choosing correctly and will live better than others.

There is a new field of study within positive psychology that focuses on psychological *resilience,* which is conceived as "the capacity to prevail in the face of adversity."[3] Several researchers have examined the way in which children, adults, and the aged have been able to cope in the face of very difficult circumstances. Children raised by mentally ill parents sometimes are able to live quite normal lives, as is the case with some children raised in extreme poverty or surrounded with the horrors of war. Some adults and older citizens were also found to be resilient in the face of extreme challenge. Parenting of a mentally ill child, loss of a job, widowhood, serious health problems all can present very difficult challenges. Some flourish despite such difficulties while others suffer disabling symptoms under the strain. Researchers are probing the various sources of strength that allow some to be resilient while others degrade under the pressure. The evidence points to things like intelligence, self-esteem, hope, optimism, community support, and so on. While Aristotle did not get this specific, he did suggest a simple basis for resilience and he called it courage, the ability to suffer hardship yet thrive in the process. The virtue of courage may have acquired a new name but, once again, the idea is still very much with us.

JUSTICE

Temperance and courage are individual and personal virtues, important to the well-being of the self. The moderate pursuit of pleasure and the endurance of some discomfort, when rightly applied, are essential to a good life. However, it is possible to imagine a temperate

[3] See Ryff, C. D., & Singer, B. Flourishing under fire: Resilience as a prototype of challenged thriving. In C. L. M. Keys & J. Haidt (Eds.). *Flourishing: Positive Psychology and the Life Well-Lived.* (2002). Washington, D.C.: American Psychological Association.

and courageous criminal. It takes courage to rob a bank and a murderer can live temperately, avoiding extravagances, so as not to draw attention to him-or herself. One can be temperate and courageous but still an awful person. The traits that enable one to moderate pleasure and pain do not in themselves make a good life. Another virtue must accompany them.

Justice is the last of what came to be known as the cardinal virtues, taken from Aristotle by the Church during the early Middle Ages. The Church fathers embraced Aristotle's views of prudence, temperance, and courage, and like The Philosopher, they recognized that the proper use of these virtues required still another virtue: justice. Aristotle called justice "chief of the virtues" and compared it to the beauty of the morning and evening star. Unfortunately, Aristotle never developed the idea of justice as well as he did the other virtues and has been criticized for his lack of clarity on the subject. But rather than focus on the problems of his discussion of justice, I would like to discuss Aristotle's main ideas, which I think are sound and generally accepted by most moral philosophers.

Temperance and courage are developed to help guide a person's behavior toward the world in general. Mastery over bodily pleasures, be they sex or alcohol or exercise, is a good thing. Similarly, the ability to withstand a little discomfort for a good cause is a necessity. Justice might be thought of as mastery over the self as it relates to other persons. Justice concerns the welfare of others; it is about fairness to others. It is truly a social virtue, a rational force controlling desire, feelings, and behavior in our everyday interaction with other people. It is not just a begrudging willingness to treat others fairly but rather a sincere desire to do so. Law professor and author Stephen Carter[4] argues, as did Aristotle, that civility is essential to democracy and to the blessings it offers.

[4] Carter, S. L. (1998). *Civility: Manners, morals, and the etiquette of democracy.* New York: Harper Collins.

In the natural world it may not be easy to find examples of fairness. It seems unfair for the bear to kill the baby deer for dinner, or the fire to ravage the forest taking the lives of countless innocent creatures, or the earthquake to devastate the homes of thousands, or the tsunami to wash away entire communities.

However, fairness does seem to be characteristic of some animals as well as human beings. We know that many animals have rules that guide their actions toward others. Darwin observed that individual turtles on the islands of Galapagos traveled toward the ocean on certain paths at apparently agreed upon times. We know that many animals develop social orders and allow certain rights to even the weakest members of the group.[5]

So, we humans are not alone in the practice of justice but we seem to have advanced far beyond what other creatures can do in this regard.

Aristotle identifies two types of justice or justice at two different levels. First, there are the agreed-upon rules developed by some form of government for the conduct of social behavior. This is the *lawful* form of justice. Aristotle assumed, perhaps incorrectly, that the *polis* (the community or the government) would develop only fair and just rules. He believed that obedience to these rules was always just. We know now that not all laws are fair and just, and at times it may be necessary to disobey an unfair law. When Rosa Parks refused to sit in the back of the bus as the unfair segregation laws required, she began the civil rights movement of the 1960s and thereby changed bad laws.

Perhaps more germane to our discussion of happiness is justice at the personal and individual level. Aristotle called it *equality.* The principle says simply "Equal rights for all, regardless of wealth or power or station in life." Children, the sick, and the weak, as well as the rich and powerful, have similar rights. Equality ensures each of

[5] Leyhausen, P. (1970). The communal organization of solitary mammals. In H. M. Proshansky, W. H. Ittelson, & L. G. Rivlin (Eds.), *Environmental psychology: Man and his physical setting.* New York: Holt, Rinehart and Winston.

us the opportunity to pursue the real goods we need to actualize our human potentials.

We must look beyond the self. We have to be concerned not only with ourselves but also with the welfare of others, not just family and friends but all others. It has been said that if we could all be true friends there would be no need for justice and we would willingly share with our dear friends. But we are not all friends. We are all human beings, however, and even the people we don't know have a right to resources important to their fulfillment. Out of our concern for them and our belief in equality, we should wish for them the same opportunities that we wish for ourselves.

In business dealings as in social interaction, fairness should prevail. The just person does not take advantage of friends nor should he take advantage of clients or partners or customers. The just person plays fairly without conflict. The just person wants to be and enjoys being fair. Fairness is a *hexis*, a habit, grounded in principles and a part of the just person's character.

From the intellectual soul and *practical wisdom*, the moral person believes in the principles of equality and fairness. Rights are to be shared; real goods ought to be accessible to all. Justice means neither taking too much nor too little. It means equality and sharing but it does not mean that we must share equally. Remember, the *golden mean* requires the right amount at the right time in the right way. Equality without regard to merit would be wrong. Rewarding the lazy in the same way as the ambitious would be unfair. The right to access does not mean "given" or "given as a gift"; we are not obligated to provide everyone with everything. Access simply means the right to pursue real goods. Justice requires us to be fair and allow others to succeed just as we wish to succeed. But it requires taking into account the circumstances. Fairness must be decided by reason. Justice considers merit as well as need.

Practical wisdom enables us to detect and evaluate the important features of each situation so that we can act wisely on principle. This virtue allows us to be fair, to be just, and to do the correct thing for others who also have the right of actualization and the need of real goods. The belief in and the practice of justice, at the personal level as well as at the legal level, allows us to live reasonably well together. We consider need and merit together. Without justice, life would be, as Thomas Hobbes suggested, "solitary, poor, nasty, brutish and short."

OTHER VIRTUES

Aristotle identified several virtues in addition to the ones discussed. To name a few, he spoke of *generosity* regarding material things and money. Some are too stingy and some are too giving, but there is a mean, a right way of giving for each of us. *Gentleness* is the control of anger. There is a time to be angry or very angry and a time not to be angry at all. There is a good way to express anger and a bad way. There are good reasons to be angry and there are bad reasons. The virtuous person knows when and how to be angry. Aristotle also spoke of *modesty*, neither boastful and flashy nor too timid and reserved. There is *pride*, neither vain nor overly humble. There are others that we need not mention here but it is important to note that the virtues go together. People who are virtuous in one area are usually virtuous in all areas of their lives. "For the presence of the single virtue of *practical wisdom* all the virtues are present."[6] Aristotle's logic here is that when *practical wisdom* is well developed, the person is able to think well about ethical and moral matters. Such a person is also good at selecting out the important features of most situations and therefore knows how to respond. If that person has acquired the principles of justice, temperance, courage, and so on, and applies them correctly to the immediate situation, then that person will be virtuous. The virtues are not learned separately as a bunch of unrelated skills. Rather,

[6] Aristotle. *Nichomachean Ethics* Book VI, Chapter 13.

the foundation of all the virtues is the same: principles, keen observation of the circumstances of the moment, and putting these together by good thinking. This explains Aristotle's view that the virtues are really unitary. They are all made possible by the same processes.[7]

Because virtue boils down to this unitary ability to integrate emotion, desire, and action with reason, I don't think it is terribly useful to identify and discuss all the virtues separately. The essence is the same for all: understanding of the principle (like fairness or gentleness or courage), keen observation of situational demands, and joining these cognitive processes with desire, feeling, and behavior. Whatever emotion or desire one has in mind, the formula is the same. Reason and pleasure we call *temperance*; reason and fear or pain we call *courage*; reason and selfishness we call *justice*.

So, what good is all this? Aristotle thinks that virtue has two sources of value. First, he believes, and I tend to agree, of course, "virtue is its own reward." That is, virtue is good in and of itself. It needs no justification. We feel good when we are virtuous, even if the outcome is less than we wished. Knowing that we did the right thing is enough.

Second, virtue is a means to fulfillment. It makes possible the acquisition of real goods. Temperance allows us to pursue long-term goals instead of short-term pleasures. Courage helps us to overcome the inevitable obstacles we meet on the way to fulfillment. Justice makes it possible to live together and to assist each other on our way to a good life.

In summary, virtue is both a prerequisite for happiness and at the same time, happiness itself. While the virtues seem to differ – one is devoted to moderating pleasure, another pain, another anger, still another selfishness – they all have common ancestors: irrational

[7] Torzynski, R. (1994). *Well-being and virtue: Investigating Aristotle's theory of eudaimonia.* Masters Thesis. Department of Psychology, California State University Fresno, Fresno, CA. An empirical study of several virtues found them to be highly correlated.

emotion, desire, and action under the guidance of reason. The virtues guide our life either in the right or in the wrong direction, depending upon how they have developed. They are the essence of the good life. They cannot receive too much attention but they can, and too often do, receive too little.

9

Virtue and Emotion

> When we react with an emotion, especially a strong one, every fiber of our being is likely to be engaged – our attention and thoughts, our needs and desires, and even our bodies.
>
> Richard S. Lazarus, *Emotion and Adaptation*, 1991, pp. 6–7 (with permission of Oxford University Press, Inc.)

We have suggested that happiness comes with fulfillment and that fulfillment requires virtue. Virtue enables us to acquire the goods we need to become all that we might.

We have also claimed that virtue may be described as *emotion moderated by reason*. The virtue of temperance allows us to moderate pleasure so that we act with the future in mind and thereby focus on real rather than apparent goods. Courage enables us to endure pain and discomfort in the present so that we may have a better future. Pain and pleasure are emotions. And so are fear, sadness, envy, jealousy, anger, and so many more. But according to Aristotle, emotion is much more than feeling. Emotion involves *thoughts, desire, and actions* as well as *feelings*. We *fear* something because we *think* it may harm us. If something is harmful we of course *want* to avoid it. Finally, we *act*; we run away from that which we think can harm us. To take another example, we are *sad* because we *know* that we have suffered a loss. We *desire* the thing that we have lost and wish its return. And we weep over our loss, as we *act* upon our feeling.

Given that emotion involves not just *feeling*, but also *thought, desire*, and *action*, the phrase "*emotion moderated by reason*" becomes

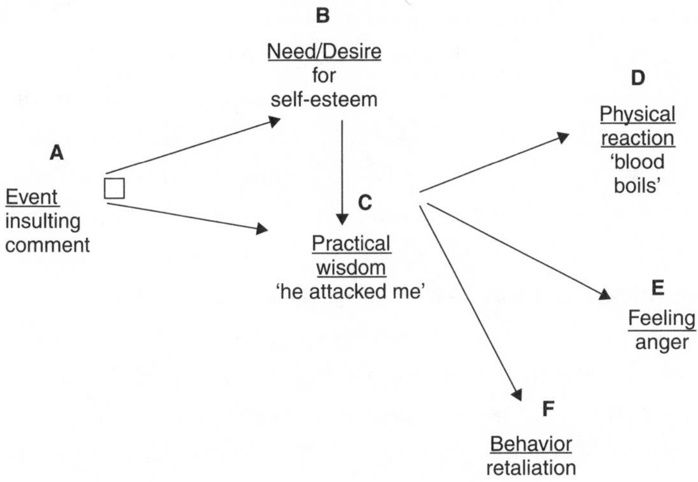

FIGURE 9.1. Aristotle's Theory of Emotion: Anger.
Source: Based upon Fortenbaugh, W.W. (2002) *Aristotle on emotion.* London: Duckworth, and Power M. & Dalgleish, T. (1997) *Cognition and emotion: from order to disorder.* Hove, East Sussex:UK: Psychology Press.

rather complicated. In order to more fully understand Aristotle's ideas about virtue we need to look more closely at his theory of emotion.[1] Figure 9.1 represents his view.

As can be seen from Figure 9.1, "emotion" for Aristotle and for many others who have followed his thinking on the matter summarizes a group of psychological processes. The figure represents the

[1] Fortenbaugh, W.W. (2002/1975) *Aristotle on emotion.* London: Duckworth. This is the best analysis of Aristotle's theory of emotion and its relationship to virtue that I have been able to find.

For further discussions of the relationship between emotion and virtue see, for example, Oakley, J. (1992). *Morality and the emotions.* New York: Routledge especially Chapters 1 and 2. Also, Sherman, N. (1997). *Making a necessity of virtue.* New York: Cambridge University Press. Sherman also discusses virtue as a learned hexis in Sherman, N. (1999). *Aristotle's ethics: Critical essays.* Lanham, MD: Rowman & Littlefield Publishers; Power, M., & Dalgleish, T. (1997) *Cognition and emotion: From order to disorder.* Hove, East Sussex: UK: Psychology Press. This book contains a brief description of Aristotle's account of emotion and several cognitive theories of emotion that followed him.

processes involved in the emotion of anger. Aristotle tells us that anger is a response to threatened self-esteem. An insult (A) begins the sequence. Also at play here is our *desire* for self-esteem (B). Without the desire for self-respect an insult wouldn't bother us but, because we do need to think well of ourselves, a threat to self-esteem makes us angry. *Practical wisdom* (C) analyzes the threat and the context in which it occurred. Recall that practical wisdom is part of the intellectual soul and, ideally, reasons well. *Practical wisdom* decides whether or not something is a threat. Depending upon the outcome of *practical wisdom's* deliberations, we carry on further with the emotional process. Modern science tells us that the sympathetic nervous system is activated (D) in preparation for defense. Our adrenal glands are invigorated and our muscles tighten, preparing for action. As our body responds we *feel* anger (E) and the desire for revenge. The physiological changes and feelings may or may not be accompanied by overt *action* (F) such as yelling or striking out at the offender.

This whole process *is* emotion. The cognitive processing of *practical wisdom*, taking into account the persons *needs and desires* as it deliberates what to do, the *physiological* changes that the body endures, the *feelings* that we are accustomed to calling "emotion," and finally the possibility of overt *action; all* are components of what Aristotle called emotion.

Central to this approach is the role of *practical wisdom*, the intellectual part of emotion. Everything depends on how our thinking assesses the situation. The effective stimulus, the actual cause of the emotion, is not the external event, the comment, as most of us are likely to believe, but rather the *thought* about the external event. What might be an insult to me and something that might set my "blood boiling" may not at all offend someone else. Emotion depends on how practical wisdom *analyzes* external events. If our reasoning determines that we were injured intentionally and wrongly, then we will experience anger and all that it entails. But if we think that the external event was said in a joking way and we decide that the insult was not really meant to offend or belittle us at all, we may smile and laugh and end it at that.

Let's consider another example. Aristotle says that fear arises when we are threatened with harm. Suppose a stranger (A) approaches you as you leave your work place. As a human being you have a need to feel safe and secure (B), (remember Maslow's safety and security need?). *Practical wisdom* (C) must deliberate the situation. Are you really in danger? Does the stranger have bad intentions toward you? If you decide that this person is a real threat, then your body will prepare itself for fight or flight (D), you will feel fear (E), and you may begin to run (E) as fast as you can. But, if you determine the stranger to be just a young person without harmful intentions, then you may simply laugh and pass by as though nothing had happened. Whether you experience fear or fun depends on how practical wisdom assesses the situation.

Most of us are accustomed to thinking of emotion as only feeling, a feeling that *happens to us* and is beyond our control. An event occurs out there in the world and causes us to be angry or afraid or jealous. We are passive victims of our emotions, which in turn depend on events in the world. But for the Ancients and for many modern philosophers and psychologists as well, the problem of emotion is much bigger than that. *Emotion is at the heart of the problem of happiness.* In the following, I discuss the relationships among happiness, emotion, and virtue.

Aristotle refers to virtue as a hexis. Hexis has been translated as "habit" but some have argued that this translation misses the mark. Habit can suggest something almost automatic and robotic, like a reflex. If true that would make virtue something far less than Aristotle claimed. He would never have imagined the virtuous person to be an unconscious robot. While there does not appear to be a good English translation of *hexis,* let's explore some possibilities.

Do you remember learning to ride a bicycle? At first it was very difficult doing so many things at once. You had to pedal, to balance, to steer, to watch out for things in your path. It took great concentration and a lot of practice to learn to ride a bicycle. You had to really think about what you were doing, but after a while this complex activity could happen with little or no conscious thought; riding a bike became a "habit." The same was probably true of learning to write your name and tie your shoes. At first it took great concentration and consciously guided motions but in time you could do these tasks easily. Complex actions turn into well-established habits, flowing freely as if they were simple actions.

But most habits are not simple actions. Their performance still depends on complex cognitive processing. You may have well-established driving habits that allow you to navigate the freeway while your thoughts are elsewhere. As the car in front of you slows, so do you, and when a car enters your lane you respond appropriately. Similarly, I am sitting at the computer and my fingers move quickly and seemingly without conscious guidance over the keyboard. Although I am not aware of what my brain is doing right now it has to be very active. My pecks at the keyboard are not the result of mindless reflexes but are guided by complex cognitive processing.

Clearly, riding a bike or driving on the freeway or typing at the keyboard cannot be compared to a simple reflex. They involve complex cognitive processing and even a certain level of conscious attention. The perfect tennis swing or the perfect swerve of the car to avoid an accident cannot be automatic. They must take into account the unique circumstances of the moment. Whether typing at the computer or avoiding an accident on the freeway – no two cases will be exactly alike. Blind, automatic, mindless habits can not be counted upon for such complicated activities. We may not be aware of what our brains are doing but common sense tells us that it is far more complex than a "knee jerk." Habits are rarely simple, automatic, robotic, mindless processes but rather are well learned, highly practiced, smooth, accurate, and refined actions that *only seem* to be automatic.[2]

Now, let's return to Aristotle's ideas on emotion. Suppose you take a new job as a salesperson, calling upon people to sell insurance or quadruple paned windows or something else they don't want. At first you are probably anxious and very uncomfortable meeting with prospective clients. But if you stay with the job long enough the anxiety will probably lessen and you will became very comfortable calling on clients and perhaps even enjoy it. I recall that when I first started teaching I was so anxious and ill at ease that I finished my first hour of lecture in just twenty minutes. I talked so fast that I ran out of things to say and had to let the class out thirty minutes early! Over the years, however, I came to feel at ease in front of a class and pretty much lost the fear that so plagued those early lectures. Every class and every lecture is different. The development of blind, automatic habits cannot explain the changes that took place over time.

Another story may help to illustrate my point. A man found a wallet in the street that contained over $250. The wallet contained ample identification and the finder, without hesitation, called and made arrangements for its return. Others upon finding such a wallet might hesitate to return it or might decide to return it less the money. But for this finder that was not a consideration. The same thing may have happened to you when a clerk gave you too much change and you unhesitatingly returned it.

What's happening here? Why did the fear and anxiety that so affected the salesperson, and me the lecturer, gradually disappear? Why did the finder of the wallet not hesitate to return it? And why did you

[2] James, W. (1893) *Psychology: Briefer course.* New York: Henry Holt and Co. Chapter 10 of this wonderful work is about habit and includes a discussion of the "practical effects of habit." James observes "First, habit simplifies our movements, makes them accurate and diminishes fatigue" as well as diminish the need for conscious attention to our actions. James' description seems a good fit with Aristotle's view of virtue.

return the excess change so quickly and so unhesitatingly? With the model presented in Figure 9.1 we can try to understand these cases.

If you noticed that Figure 9.1 looks a lot like virtue, where reason moderates feelings and leads to adaptive and effective behavior, you are right. Virtue and emotion are not only similar; they are almost the same thing. When emotion is viewed as Aristotle conceived it, a complex of psychological processes including but not restricted to feeling, then emotion and virtue merge.

Figure 9.1 shows that *practical wisdom*, taking into account the needs and desires of the person, analyzes the event: Is there a threat or not? Do I need to be afraid? Let's return to the salesperson. The first call was the hardest. The salesperson, like all of us, has the desire to be well thought of and to maintain self-esteem. Upon making the first call, the salesperson didn't know what to expect. The second call got a little more predictable, the third and forth even more so, and gradually, as the salesperson came to analyze the situations more accurately, the threat of rejection diminished and so did the fear. *Practical wisdom* became familiar with "making a sales call" and the sales presentations became better and better until they were almost "automatic." "Making a sales call" was becoming a habit. In time the salesperson could call upon a client without any anxiety at all. The same explanation can be offered for the gradual decrease in fear as the lecturer became more experienced. As *practical wisdom* became more familiar with the classroom setting, the threat of embarrassment decreased and so did anxiety. Practical wisdom gradually masters the task of selling or lecturing and now guides feelings, physiological activity, and behavior as though it were just a simple act. A set of very complex processes has become a habit or as Aristotle would say a *hexis*.

The same analysis may be used in the instance of the customer who received too much change. The customer had the desire to be honest (justice, in Aristotelian terms) and upon discovering the error simply put the required actions into play. Upon analyzing the situation and respecting the desire, *practical wisdom* simply returned the money: no conflict, no hesitation, and no second thoughts. It seemed so automatic, but practical wisdom's complex processing was still very much in play.

Recall that practical wisdom is an intellectual virtue with reasoning at its core. It must think well, observe circumstances, and monitor needs. It must control feelings and the bodily processes related to feelings, as well as steer behavior. *Hexis* may simply mean that this whole complex action has become refined, accurate, and efficient and no longer requires vigilant conscious attention. Complex mental processing is occurring but it has been so well practiced and has become so refined that normal levels of consciousness are unnecessary. Now it is time to connect such habits as we have been describing, with virtue. In Book II, 6 of the *Ethics* Aristotle reminds us that:

> If virtue, like nature, requires more accuracy and is better than any art, then it will aim at the mean. I speak of *moral virtue*, since that is concerned with *emotions and actions.*

Moral virtue is concerned with *emotions and actions*! Figure 9.1 tells us that emotions and actions are part of the same process. Actions flow from *practical wisdom*, desire, feelings, and physiological activity, the whole of which Aristotle called "emotion." There is a unity about us; actions, feelings, glandular activity, thinking, and even desire are all part and parcel of this unified process Aristotle called "emotion."

It is possible for this unified process to become so well learned and so practiced that it can run itself with little or no conscious awareness. When the salesperson gained experience in calling on clients, when the lecturer became accustomed to the classroom, and when the patron at the store returned the excess change to the clerk, feeling and action required little or no conscious thought. Emotion/behavior had become a *hexis*, a habit. *Practical wisdom* may occur at the conscious level but, as we will see in Chapter 11, it can also go on without awareness.

When "emotions and actions" that "aim at the mean" become so well established that they can occur on the spot, suddenly, and without the benefit of effortful thinking, then they have become a *hexis*. It may be alright to translate that as "habit" as long as it includes the complicated kind of activities that we have reviewed. When we are in the habit of doing things right, desiring the mean, feeling neither too little nor too much, and behaving correctly, then we have become virtuous. Virtue covers it all – desiring, thinking, feeling, and acting correctly to get the real goods we need for fulfillment. Remember, that is what it's all about. To be fulfilled we need real goods and virtue makes that possible. When all the pieces of virtue (good thinking, desire, feeling, action) come together "naturally" and with little effort, when they flow smoothly and accurately as if they were "second nature," then they have become a *hexis*. And, when that happens we are on our way to *eudaimonia*.

10

Early Psychological Views of Virtue and Emotion

Habit is thus the enormous fly-wheel of society, its most precious conservative agent.

William James (1900) *Principles of Psychology*

Aristotle's view of emotion is actually the prototype of what psychologists now call the "cognitive theory of emotion." There are currently several variations of this approach, some of which will be reviewed in the next chapter. However, the earlier classical approaches to emotion offered by Sigmund Freud and William James are still important and deserving of some discussion.

Terms like "moral virtue", "practical wisdom," "soul," and the like, were dropped from all but philosophical discourse a long time ago.[1] But the ideas to which these terms refer are still very much with us. "Virtue ethics" has always been a part of psychology. In the following pages I discuss emotion and virtue from a psychological point of view rather than in the terms of philosophy.

It seems appropriate to begin with the most famous of all psychologists, Sigmund Freud. Freud was a scholar of many disciplines

[1] Fowers, B.J. (2005) *Virtue and psychology: Pursuing excellence in ordinary practices.* Washington, D.C. American Psychological Association. Fowers book is an exception to the rule. It offers a review of Aristotle's ideas on virtue and practical wisdom and discusses them in the context of the practice of clinical psychology. Schwartz, B., & Sharpe, K.E. (2006). Practical wisdom: Aristotle meets positive psychology. *Journal of Happiness Studies. 7*, 377–395 is a recent article that also introduces practical wisdom in the context of theory and research in positive psychology.

and familiar with Ancient Greek thought. Greek terms like *ego, Eros*, and *Oedipus* are fundamental to his theory.[2] One of Freud's most important contributions was his re-statement of Plato's analysis of soul. Two thousand years ago Plato divided the human soul into three parts: the *appetitive*, the *spirited*, and the *rational*. Of course, appetite refers to desire and needs. The *spirited* part of Plato's soul referred to the action/behavior of many living things symbolized by the spirited horse. Finally, Plato identified the most important part of the human soul, the capacity to reason. In a psychologically healthy person the rational part of the soul is dominant. Plato used the metaphor of a Greek chariot with reason at the reins, driving the *appetitive* and *spirited* horses. Reason must be in charge of both desire and behavior. Plato said this even before Aristotle.

Freud changed the words but kept Plato's ideas. First, the term "soul," having taken on religious meaning during the Middle Ages, was replaced with "personality." For Freud the *ego* was the rational part of the personality and, in the healthy individual, it keeps the *id* and *superego* in check. The *id* refers to our child-like unconscious desires, similar to Plato's *appetite*. The *superego* represents our largely unconscious ideas about morality passed from parents and culture and the source of our guilt. The desires of the *id* can lead to thoughts and actions involving sex and aggression, the two basic motives of the personality. The *superego*, developed in childhood, will most likely attempt to thwart those desires and actions and even punish the personality for thinking about such acts. Both the *id* and *superego* are largely irrational and immature and must be controlled by reason, by the *ego*, just as they were in Plato and in Aristotle. In Freud's writings "virtue" assumed a different name; it became a "strong *ego*." But despite the name change we have a similar story; reason pursues mastery over the irrational parts of the personality. Plato and Aristotle passed to a new age.

[2] Hall, G. S. (1954/1961). *A primer of Freudian psychology*. New York: Mentor Books.

At the time Freud was developing his psychoanalytic view of personality, William James published his *Principles of Psychology*.[3] The *Principles* has been described as the best thing ever written in psychology,[4] and I tend to agree with that assessment. James came to be called a moral psychologist and I understand that to mean that William James, like Aristotle, was concerned with using psychological principles to improve the quality of life. I will briefly touch on a few of James' ideas before reviewing his thoughts on emotion, which are central to virtue and happiness.

William James urged us to develop good habits (remember the Greek *hexis*?) in our youth. He called habit the great "flywheel of society."[5] Once a habit is established it tends to go on and on, like a flywheel goes round and round, and carries us through much of life, even without awareness. James, in his wonderful Victorian prose, says "it keeps the fisherman and the deckhand at sea through the winter; it holds the miner in his darkness, and nails the countryman to his log cabin and his lonely farm through all the months of snow." James tries to scare us into developing good habits in our youth because "by the age of thirty, the character has set like plaster, and will never soften again." Perhaps a little exaggerated but most agree that it's easier to learn good habits when we are young.

James also wrote a wonderful chapter on will. He observed that conscious thought never stops but is like a stream that flows on, without breaks or divisions. But we do have the ability to extract a thought as it passes through consciousness, and if we hold the

[3] James' *Psychology: The Briefer Course* (1892/1961; London: Collier Books), written as a textbook for his students at Harvard, is a smaller and easier to read version of the original *Principles*.

[4] MacLeod, R. B. (Ed.) (1969). *William James: Unfinished Business*. Washington D.C. American Psychological Assoc.

[5] James, W. *Psychology: The Briefer Course* (1892/1961). See especially Chapters 10 (Habit) and 26 (Will) and Chapter 12 (The Self). See Chapters 24 and 25 on emotion and instinct.

thought in mind, keeping it "before the footlights of consciousness," it will grow in strength and eventually express itself in behavior. For example, if we keep the thought of exercise in our minds long enough and in varied ways, we will eventually act on it. It was James' "ideo-motor" theory. An *idea* that is held in consciousness grows stronger and more powerful and eventually is carried out in *motor* action. It's a wonderfully useful idea and not unrelated to Aristotle's notion of virtue and the power of reason over emotion and behavior.

Still another contribution of William James to the issue of happiness can be found in his chapter on self. James offers the following equation:

$$\text{SELF-ESTEEM} = \frac{\text{SUCESSES}}{\text{PRETENTIONS}}$$

By "successes" James might include advances toward actualization and fulfillment. By "pretensions" James refers to those *things that we think we should be but don't really care to be.* "How pleasant is the day when we give up striving to be young, or slender! Thank God! We say, *those* illusions are gone." According to James, self-esteem (this is really close to happiness) is determined by the ratio of successes to pretensions. Happiness grows by increasing fulfillment *and* by minimizing false goals or pretensions. Reducing goals to just those you truly care about boosts your well-being just as much as goal accomplishment. The moral is… concentrate on those goals that matter and free yourself from those that are merely pretentions.

Most important for our discussion of virtue is William James' view on emotion, which has influenced the study of emotion for over one hundred years. Simply put, James thought that emotion has two sides. First is the physiological side; second is the experiential or feeling side. When we feel an emotion our experience is always accompanied by physiological activity. Our glands are pumping, nerves are firing, and hearts are racing. For James every emotion has a unique set of bodily, physiological processes at its core. Fear has a different set of physiological underpinnings than anger; sadness has different underlying glandular and nervous actions than anxiety.

Most people believe that feeling comes first, which in turn leads to the physiological changes. As James put it, most believe that (a) we see a bear, (b) we feel afraid, and (c) then we tremble and run. We feel first and have bodily and physiological activity second.

James wrote his *Principles of Psychology* just forty years after Darwin published his *The Origin of Species* and just a year after his *Expressions of Emotion in Men and Animals.* James was very taken with Darwin's emphasis on instinct and used it in his theory of emotion. While James is not entirely clear about why our body reacts as it does, he believes that instinct plays a role. If a child sees a snarling dog, his heart races and his body is put on high alert. *The child now feels the activity in his body and this feeling* is *the emotion.* For William James then, we *feel what the body is doing.*

Why does the body react before the feeling? Why do we run when we see a bear? Why does the child fear the snarling dog? Instinct has something to do with it but James also stresses the importance of learning and experience. There is interplay between the two which makes it easy for a *hexis* to develop.

The cat may chase the mouse instinctively the first time, but after that first encounter memory will always be in play to influence the action. After the first instance pure instinct is gone; instinct and experience now meld together as one. Contemporary psychology offers a similar idea called "*preparedness.*" Psychologist Martin Seligman[6] reminds us of how common it is to have a fear of heights, closed places, snakes and other creepy crawly things, despite the fact that very few of us have ever taken a serious fall from a high place or been bitten by a snake. We are more likely to have fallen from a bicycle than a ladder, yet few if any of us fear a bicycle. Seligman suggests that we are biologically *prepared* to learn responses, especially emotional reactions,

[6] Seligman, M. (1971). Phobias and preparedness. *Behavior Therapy*, 2, 307–320.

to certain stimuli and situations. It is evolutionarily adaptive to be afraid of heights and creepy things. Learning emotional and behavioral responses to these things is easy, rapid, and long lasting. The fear of snakes can quickly become a habit, a *hexis* consisting of both instinctive and learned ingredients.

Let's look at how an emotional *hexis* might work. Suppose you are driving down a residential street and a child runs out in front of you to retrieve a ball. You slam on the breaks and stop just in time. The child gets the ball and runs off to resume playing. A couple of blocks down the road you feel yourself getting fearful as you sense your body trembling and your heart racing. What's happening here?

You "automatically" stopped the car to avoid something terrible. Your body acted as it knew how, as the *hexis* required. Messages were sent to all parts of the body to react appropriately. Then, as you began to sense your bodily activity, you became emotional. The body acted, then the mind perceived those bodily processes and experienced feeling. Had the situation been different, a different set of physiological processes would have been set in motion and a different emotion would have been felt.

William James is probably best known for his philosophy of pragmatism, the idea that usefulness is a major criterion for truthfulness. We can accept something as true, at least temporarily, if it works. James was very good at thinking of ways to *make use* of an idea to test its validity. Bodily responses come first, before the feeling, and are the very basis of the feeling. Therefore, if you want to feel a certain way, guide your body to act that way! I call this idea "whistle a happy tune." If you are feeling blue and want to get over it – do something! "Whistle a happy tune"; smile, go to a party, go to a funny movie. Get your body to act as though you feel good and you will feel good. "Act the way you want to feel." Initiate a *hexis* to counteract the state in which you find yourself. Let reason guide you to feeling better. *Reason guides actions and actions are always accompanied by physiological activity. Physiology determines feeling. Hexes* can be brought into play by the outside world or by thinking. Reason can guide action and emotion just as external conditions bring them about. Sounds a little like Aristotle's virtue!!

James may not have the whole answer but his idea that emotion is a feeling, grounded in physiology and often brought about "automatically" as a *hexis,* has had a very long run in psychology and is reasonably consistent with the Aristotelian view of emotion. In recent years, however, a more complex Aristotelian view has pretty much overtaken the Jamesian rendition. Aristotle's theory of emotion was the original cognitive view and has, as we will see in the following chapter, inspired several recent theoretical variations with different levels of complexity and precision.

11

Virtue and Emotion: Recent Psychological Views

> Why, then, 'tis none to you; for there is nothing either good or bad, but thinking makes it so.
>
> Act 2, Scene 2 of Shakespeare's *Hamlet*

There are a number of developments in contemporary psychology that have embraced Aristotle's view of virtue and its importance to a good life. In this chapter I will discuss some recent variations of Aristotle's virtue/emotion theory and how they have been used to treat unhappiness. Although unhappiness is not the main concern of this book, it is to some degree the flip side of our primary interest, and an understanding of one can add to our knowledge of the other.

Cognitive psychology started to blossom in the 1960s as Behaviorism's grip on the discipline weakened. Recognizing the value of John Watson's claim that he could make each of us a "doctor, lawyer, artist, merchant-chief and, yes, even beggar-man and thief" by controlling the environment, and also acknowledging Freud's idea that human problems stem from irrational motives and childhood trauma, cognitive psychology offered still another view – a return to Aristotle.

ALBERT ELLIS'S ABC MODEL

Albert Ellis, one of the early cognitive therapists, proposed that we usually feel the way we think. Therefore, changing thoughts can change feelings! Ellis and his colleagues summarize this idea in their ABC model.[1]

Irrational beliefs often lay behind our suffering and unhappiness. By becoming more rational we improve our lives. Ellis's treatment program began as rational therapy (RT) but realizing the centrality of emotion and behavior, it eventually became rational emotive behavior therapy or REBT. Just as Aristotle did, Ellis recognized the unbreakable ties among thinking, emotion, and behavior. REBT was one of the first cognitive therapies and is still widely used to help people live more satisfying lives (Figure 11.1).

In the ABC model mentioned above, "A" stands for an activating event like a conflict at work. "B" refers to thoughts and beliefs about the event. As noted in Chapter 9, experience is not necessarily a copy of an event but rather an interpretation. "C" refers to the consequences of "A and B." In this case a supervisor scolded (A) Mike who interpreted it (B) as a failure on his part and responded (C) by becoming depressed. A co-worker Bill was similarly mistreated (A) but thought of it as just another of the boss's outbursts on a difficult day. He didn't like being berated but thought of it (B) as the boss's problem, not his. The consequences (C) are very different for the two co-workers because of their different interpretations of the incident. Bill has a healthy reaction to the event and suffers no serious consequences.

Ellis suggests that most of our basic or *core beliefs*, those that impact us in many ways on a daily basis, operate at an unconscious level. We establish rules about how things should be, how we should be, how others should be, and how the world should be. Incoming sensory events are compared to these beliefs and a reaction results.

Jason's idea that he must always do well and never fail is irrational. Even the threat of failure makes Jason anxious, but it is irrational to think that he can always succeed. If Jason can accept that he

[1] Ellis, A., & Harper R. A. (1961/1997). *A guide to rational living.* North Hollywood, CA: Wilshire Book Company.

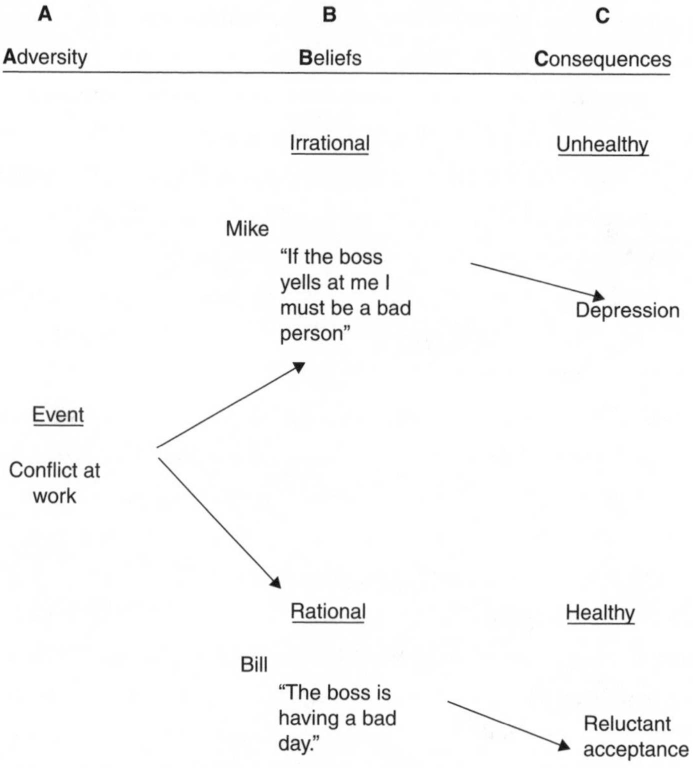

Figure 11.1. The Albert Ellis REBT Model of Emotion.

is good at some things but not so good at others, and that it is okay to be that way, then anxiety over failure disappears. A single belief change can prevent an anxious reaction to hundreds of situations.

Jane has an irrational belief that she must always be comfortable and secure, and becomes very anxious when she is not. Too hot, too cold, too much to do, too little help from others all cause Jane to be anxious. Eventually Jane structures her world to preserve her comfort. Her *core belief* now controls her life. *Core beliefs* often become demands. We demand of ourselves, of others, and of the world that things go our way so that we can be free of anxiety. How much better for Jane if she could change her *core beliefs* to include discomfort as a part of life, everyone's life? "Yes, it is hot but I can take it." "I have too much to do now but I'll survive." Simple but rational thoughts like these can change our lives dramatically.

The goal of REBT is to change destructive, controlling, irrational beliefs. Once that is accomplished, a huge range of situations that once caused misery become just bothersome. One little change in thinking can solve hundreds of problems.

Ellis's therapeutic techniques are designed to make a client aware of the irrationality of his or her thinking and thereby begin the development of new and more adaptive beliefs. To the client suffering from unrequited love, Ellis may point out that there is no law of the universe that love must be reciprocated. The loss of a job is not the end of the world, nor is the loss of friendship. Life is full of hardships but we must learn to see them for what they are – hardships, not devastating crises. To clients who think they are terrible people because they did a bad thing, Ellis may point out the important difference between actions and the self. We can do bad things for many reasons, including ignorance, thoughtlessness, or inattention. If bad actions were always performed by bad people, we would all be bad people. Ellis tells us to repeat over and over to ourselves, until we believe it: "I'm never a fool, even though I may do foolish things." Along these lines Ellis and his colleagues have developed exercises and homework assignments so that we can rid *ourselves* of those powerful irrational thoughts that abuse us day after day.[2]

If we refer back to Chapter 9 and view the figure of Aristotle's model of emotion, it is easy to see the similarities between what Aristotle called *practical wisdom*, and what Ellis called "thoughts and beliefs" in the ABC model. For both the ancient philosopher and the cognitive therapist it is the thought not the external event that causes emotion. Although twenty-five hundred years apart and with

[2] Walen, S. R., DiGiuseppe, R., & Wessler, R. L. (1980). *A practitioner's guide to rational emotive therapy*. New York: Oxford University Press.

slightly different language, the idea is the same. Reason remains the instrument by which we moderate feelings and actions.

RICHARD LAZARUS' APPRAISAL THEORY OF EMOTION

We get emotional over things we care about. Another glance at Figure 9.1 will reveal that needs and desires are integral parts of emotion. If we didn't care about, want, or desire, a positive self image then an insult would have little effect upon us. If we didn't care about supporting a family then losing a job may not trouble us. We show little emotion over things we don't care about.

Richard Lazarus[3] takes this fact as a starting point and suggests that when a need or desire has been satisfied, or is expected to be satisfied, we feel positive emotion. And when a need is frustrated or likely to be, we feel negative emotion. Emotion depends upon the state of needs. When people or events in the world are kind to us and fulfill our needs we feel good, but when our desires are frustrated we feel bad. Both positive and negative emotions occur in relation to needs, just as Aristotle claimed.

Because needs are so central to emotion it is very useful to *know* how they work. For Lazarus, that means we must *appraise* how something, say another person or an event, will impact a need. Other people and events are only the indirect cause of emotional reactions. The direct cause is the estimate of how our needs will be affected. Remember, emotions don't just happen to us as we passively take in the world. It is our thoughts that matter to emotion. If we *think* that something can harm us we are likely to feel one of the negative emotions like fear, anger, anxiety, shame, sadness, envy, jealousy, or disgust. If we *think* that something will benefit us we will feel a positive emotion like pride, relief, or love. But

[3] Lazarus, R. S. (1991). *Emotion and adaptation*. New York: Oxford University Press.

ultimately it is our appraisal of the situation that is responsible for our emotion.

Lazarus splits the process of appraisal into two stages. First, we must judge if something is relevant to our needs. If we don't really care about the graffiti that seems to be popping up in our neighborhoods then it is not likely to upset us. But if we think that our security is being threatened by gangs and that the value of our home is in jeopardy, then we will be afraid. The point is that we must make a judgment about whether an event will impact our needs before we become emotional about it.

Lazarus notes that a second form of appraisal also occurs. The person must judge how he or she will be able to cope with the event. If the problem can be easily solved then the intensity of the emotion will be only slight. But, if the person believes that his or her life is under threat and that it will be difficult to ward off the threat, the emotional reaction can be extreme.

Lazarus elaborates on the basic Aristotelian model even further by suggesting two forms of coping strategies. We might deal with a threat by active problem solving. For example, in the case of the graffiti, one might go to the police or try and find the kids responsible to report it to their parents. But another way to cope with a threat might be to change one's appraisal. A friend might suggest that the graffiti in the area is just the work of a few teenagers, unrelated to gangs, and presents no danger to anyone. Should our potential victim be convinced of this argument then he or she could easily cope with the situation. A change in appraisal reduces the threat and the emotion. Thus, we can change the way we feel by *acting* on the world to change events or we can change the way we *think* about the events. Of course, there is an appropriate time for each but Lazarus instructs us that our emotional lives are changeable and his therapy is mainly directed toward modifying appraisal tendencies.[4]

[4] Lazarus, R. S., & Lazarus, B. N. (1994). *Passion and reason: Making sense of our emotions.* New York: Oxford University Press.

We can't help but notice here that what Lazarus refers to as emotional coping seems to be at the very heart of Aristotle's idea of virtue. Virtue is the influence of reason upon feeling and acting. Once again, old wine in a new bottle.

THE POWER AND DALGLEISH MODEL

Psychologists Mick Power and Tim Dalgleish have elaborated the cognitive theories of emotion and moved them toward even more precision.[5] Their model suggests that appraisal takes place on several levels and at various degrees of consciousness. They call their theory the SPAARS approach where the letters S, P, A, A, R, S refer to different kinds of mental processes that occur during appraisal. I would like to simplify things a bit by using simpler terms to describe the various kinds of processing. The simplified model is presented in Figure 11.2.

Events in the world can be represented in the mind in the form of pictures, smells, sounds, tastes, and so on. You probably can imagine or picture your front door or the tree in your back yard quite easily. You can probably "hear" a tune that you remember from childhood. These are sensory images or memories that we carry in our minds either at the conscious or unconscious level. Events in the world are also represented in the form of language. You can probably describe a remembered event with just a few words. Language memories needn't be in good English or Spanish or French, but are often just "natural language" that captures the meaning of some event in the simplest way. My grandson has a wonderful talent for expressing himself clearly in less than perfect English. "Jack no like" is clear enough to all.

These mental representations of events in the world are joined with information from our needs and knowledge of the world

[5] Power, M., & Dalgleish, T. (1997). *Cognition and emotion: From order to disorder.* Hove, East Susses, UK: Psychology Press.

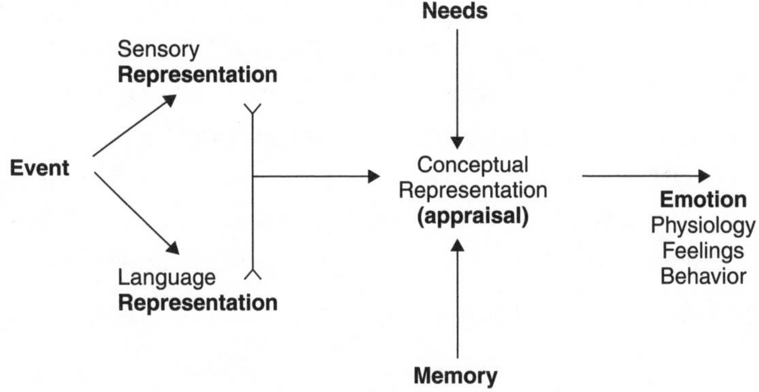

Figure 11.2. Simplified SPAARS Model of Emotion.
Source: Power, M., & Dalgleish, T. (1997) *Cognition and emotion: From order to disorder.* Hove, East Sussex, UK: Psychology Press.

to form a conceptual representation of the event. This conceptual representation is what Power and Dalgleish call the appraisal. They use an example of a jogger who comes across a bear in the woods where she is jogging. The bear is the event and is represented by a visual image in the jogger's mind and also by a crude kind of language like "bear, big, strong, hurt me." These images then combine with the jogger's knowledge and memory of bears and with her needs and goals, like the need for survival. The coming together of the bear's mental (pictorial and language) representations with the jogger's knowledge of bears, and her needs, desires, and goals, results in a cognitive appraisal of the situation. She determines that the bear could hurt or even kill her. She experiences fear. Fear, of course, is more than a feeling; it includes the mental processes described here as well as changes in the body's physiology, the awareness of danger, and most likely some kind of flight response like running away.

Power and Dalgleish tell us that while we are usually at least somewhat aware of our mental representations and our appraisals, it is not unusual for all of these things to occur at an unconscious level. We can become afraid without awareness of our mental representations, our memories, or even our appraisals. We can feel angry or sad and not know why. As we will see in Chapter 12, emotions take place in several areas of the brain and may remain entirely at the unconscious level. All of us have had the experience of feeling fear or anger but not understanding why. Our sensory and language mental representations and even our appraisals can take place without conscious awareness and leave us at a loss to explain why we feel the way we do. Emotions are, as we have seen, much more complicated than most of us believed.

VIRTUE AS CONSTRUCTIVE THINKING

Psychologist Seymour Epstein believes that unconscious processing is the key to understanding emotions in general. He proposes that we humans have two minds.[6] The first is the familiar rational and conscious mind, the one that the Ancient Greeks so admired. It analyzes, deliberates, thinks in terms of causes and effects, and in general reasons well. It understands Aristotle's syllogisms.

The other mind is only partially conscious and only partially rational. The *experiential mind* learns directly from experience rather than from reasoning. Thinking about an engineering problem requires the use of symbols like numbers and relationships expressed in words. But such mental content may not be found in an adult's memory of childhood abuse. The emotional experience and feelings are what is remembered and these may be re-lived despite repeated attempts at rational control. The *experiential mind* lacks the rationality of the mind we are accustomed to. It operates automatically and can resist attempts at control. It thinks quickly, sometimes carelessly, and is less accurate and precise than the conscious mind but it can serve us well when "on the spot" judgments are required. The *experiential mind* allows us to "shoot from the hip."

[6] Epstein, S., & Meier, P. (1989). Constructive thinking: A broad coping variable with specific components. *Journal of Personality and Social Psychology 57*, 332–350.

It is more intuitive than our rational mind and, most important in this context, it is the origin of most of our emotions. "*Your experiential mind* not only interprets events but also seeks to manage the emotions you feel. ... The more emotionally aroused you are, be it severe stress, frustrations, fear, anger, or even ecstatic pleasure, the more you come under the sway of your *experiential mind*."[7]

When the *experiential mind* and the rational mind work well together they produce what Epstein refers to as *constructive thinking*. Constructive thinking is defined as "the degree to which a person's *automatic thinking* ... facilitates solving problems in everyday life at a minimum cost in stress." Sometimes we have to think and act quickly without time to deliberate, and if our two minds cooperate we will do well, even without the benefit of conscious processing. In a word, Epstein's constructive thinking is *habitual* good thinking that requires no conscious guidance. Good thinking is that which has been practiced, is well established, and no longer needs the guidance of the rational mind. Favorable experiences have allowed the *experiential mind* to store adaptive emotions and actions and these responses are now second nature. Habitual and automatic good thinking now can produce appropriate emotions and constructive actions. Said differently, the *experiential mind* "knows" the right thing to do and when to do it.

Epstein's constructive thinking sounds an awful lot like virtue! When virtue became "second nature" and habitual, Aristotle called it a *hexis* to feel and do the right thing at the right time. The ability to find the *golden mean* easily and with little effort becomes part of our character and flows freely.

> The mean and the good is feeling at the right time, about the right things in relation to the right people, for the right reason; and the mean and the good are the task of virtue. Similarly, in regard to actions there are excesses, deficiency, and the mean.

[7] Epstein, S. (1998). *Constructive thinking: The key to emotional intelligence*. Westport, CT: Praeger, pp. 72, 102–3, 136.

Remember from Chapter 9 how *practical wisdom* integrated information from an event (such as an insult) and our needs/desires (such as the need for self-esteem), and how *practical wisdom* was actually an intellectual virtue guided by reason and logic. But over time, as emotions and actions were practiced and became habitual, *practical wisdom* played less and less of a role. Epstein's constructive thinking operates the same way. As the *experiential mind* develops from life experiences it gradually increases its control over our lives. It comes to guide our emotions and actions automatically and without the necessity of rational thinking. Doesn't that resonate of Aristotle's virtue, which eventually becomes "natural" and effortless with time? It becomes a *hexis*, part of our character.

To assess a person's ability to do *constructive thinking* Epstein has developed a psychological test called the Constructive Thinking Inventory or CTI.[8] The CTI consists of several statements that may or may not be true of the person who rates them. For example, one statement says "I don't worry about things I can do nothing about." Another is "There are basically two kinds of people in the world, good and bad." A third reads "I don't feel that I have to perform exceptionally well in order to consider myself a worthwhile person." Each statement is rated for its truth or falsity relative to that person. The test items can be divided into several categories but a few categories seem especially important. *Emotional coping* measures how well a person deals with his or her emotions; the ability to take failure, disapproval, and negative emotions in stride. *Behavioral coping* measures how adaptively a person acts in day-to-day dealings with the world, the willingness to plan, and be realistic. *Categorical thinking* and *superstitious thinking* measures how much the person is burdened by or free from erroneous and immature types of thinking.

Over many years Epstein has found a strong connection between constructive thinking and several measures of successful living. His

[8] Epstein, S., & Brodsky, A. (1993). *You're smarter than you think.* New York: Simon & Shuster.

studies include "super achievers" who have attained great financial success. These subjects scored higher on the CTI than a group of "average executives." Not only were these people successful in their work lives but in their personal lives as well. "Super achievers spend more time with their spouses and children and are somewhat more satisfied with their marital, sex, family and social lives than average executives." Similar results emerged from Epstein's studies of school administrators, naval officers, and insurance agents. College students who scored higher on the CTI were found to be more successful at work and enjoyed greater job satisfaction than students with lower CTI scores. In his studies IQ score was correlated with academic success but did not predict work performance at all, as did the CTI. Epstein also found evidence to support the effect of constructive thinking on well-being and happiness. He states "Overall, the research my associates and I did with the Constructive Thinking Inventory provides compelling evidence that the more constructively you think, the happier you feel, and the better your emotional adjustment." Our own studies with the CTI obtained similar results.[9] The CTI correlated very highly with our measures of virtue and well-being. It appears that Epstein's constructive thinking is another way of looking at what Aristotle called virtue. And, in our studies, the CTI and tests designed to measure virtue were highly correlated. Both were predictive of well being. Constructive thinking, in other words, is a modern term for virtue.

Aristotle's concept of virtue is very much alive and well in contemporary psychology. Virtue can be thought of as the moderation of emotion by reason. It is a premise of the new cognitive psychology that external events are not really the cause of emotions or actions.

[9] Franklin, S., & Torzynski, R. (1993). Virtue and well-being: Evidence for Aristotle's eudaemonic theory of happiness. Paper presented at the Meeting of the Western Psychological Association. Phoenix, AZ.
Franklin, S. (1994). An examination of Aristotle's concept of virtue and its relationship to well-being. Paper presented at the Meeting of the Western Psychological Association. Los Angeles.

It is rather the mental interpretation of the event that is causal. We no longer believe that we are passive recipients of emotion and at its mercy. Aristotle painted a much more complicated, but more reasonable picture of emotion and we have finally caught up with him.

Albert Ellis was an early cognitive therapist and offered the ABC model of emotion. Ellis stressed the importance and the power of the belief or thought that comes between the external event and the feeling. He showed us that we can change how we feel by changing the thought. Richard Lazarus elaborated the message and suggested that the intervening thought processes occur in two stages. First we must decide if an event even matters to us and if it will affect our needs in some way, either positively or negatively. Then, if we decide that an event might be harmful we must decide whether or not we can cope with it. Lazarus distinguished two types of coping, behavioral and emotional. Emotional coping is simply altering our interpretation of an event. If we decide that something that we judged as threatening is really not so serious as originally thought, we reduce our discomfort just as if we altered the event itself.

Power and Dalgleish elaborated the model even further by showing that interpretation takes place in two forms: sensory and language. And, in appraising an event, both our needs and our memory of similar events come into play.

Finally, Epstein's theory of constructive thinking proposed that our interpretations and appraisals are usually performed at an unconscious level. Epstein advised that the more our interpretations become habitual and automated (*hexes*), the more effective they can be and the more able we are to cope with the world. Ellis, Lazarus, Power and Dalgleish, and Epstein are all strikingly similar to Aristotle. Virtue may have some new names but "a rose by any other name is still a rose."

12

The Physiological Basis of Virtue

> Improved understanding of emotion in the brain will pave the way for understanding of the self, personality and social behavior.
>
> Joseph LeDoux (1998)

Darwin believed that most emotion was instinctive and had survival value. William James refined the idea suggesting that each emotion had a distinctive set of bodily reactions that are the basis of feelings. Anger has one set of physiological processes, fear another, joy still another, and so on. For James the bodily response instinctively occurs, and then as we become aware of what our bodies are doing, we feel emotions. The physiological reaction occurs *prior to feeling.*

The Jamesian theory still has merit, as we will show later in this chapter, and may well be useful in explaining emotion among the lower animals. However, our human brains have become very complicated structures and allow other mechanisms for emotion as well. By taking a brief journey into the human brain we may come to more fully understand emotion and what Aristotle called virtue: its moderation by reason.

Our brains can be divided into roughly three parts (Figure 12.1). The most primitive *"reptilian" brain* is the oldest division and is

---

Epigraph. Joseph LeDoux, Closing Session of the Future of the Study of Emotion 2000. NIMH Conference May, 1998 Permission by personal communication with Joseph LeDoux.

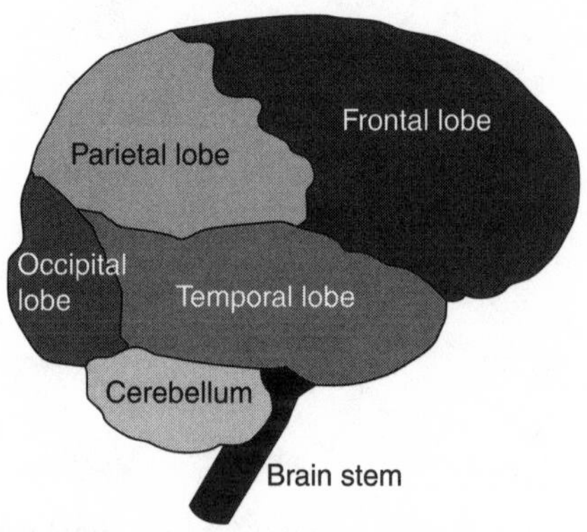

FIGURE 12.1. The human brain as seen from the right; the lobes of the cerebral cortex and the cerebellum.

found in both lower animals and primates. Sometimes called the brain stem, this area is responsible for basic life functions: breathing, heartbeat, body temperature, balance, and the like.

The *cerebellum* is also evolutionarily very old and relatively primitive. It houses the *limbic system,* a group of structures deeply involved in emotion.

Finally, there is the *cerebral cortex*, the largest, and in some ways, most important part of the human brain. This cerebral cortex sits atop the other structures and is divided into sections or *lobes* as well as into halves or hemispheres. The frontal lobes of each hemisphere are centers for reasoning, planning, problem solving, and some emotional activity. The parietal lobes are associated with movement and some perceptual activities. The occipital lobes are often called the visual centers, although they are really only one of many places in the brain that process visual information. Lastly, there are the temporal lobes where auditory perception, speech, and some memory occur. These lobes, making up the *cerebral cortex*, are found only in mammals and are most highly developed in primates.

Recent neurological studies have revealed some truly fascinating things about how the areas of the human brain work together.[1] Remember that Aristotle suggested that virtue is the moderation of emotion by reason. Although it took 2,500 years, we now have neurological evidence that he was right.

Figure 12.2 is a diagram of an emotional process at the neurological level. A potentially dangerous object or event occurs, which in the illustration is a snake. The snake is detected by the eyes and an impulse is sent to the thalamus, which is a kind of clearing house for all incoming sensory information. The thalamus sends the information over two routes. First to a structure called the *amygdala* (there are actually two amygdalae, one in each hemisphere), which is located in the limbic system. The amygdala is a primitive part of the brain, which gathers memories of emotional experiences from the past and compares them with incoming information. The amygdala also receives information from the hippocampus, which stores settings and contexts and compares them with current conditions. Thus, not only is the snake detected but the context in which it is found is also noted. The amygdala will respond very differently to a snake that makes a sudden appearance in the backyard and a snake behind glass at the zoo. The hippocampus knows the difference between these settings and the amygdala uses that information to react accordingly. If the amygdala "judges" a situation to be dangerous it has

[1] Recent research on the role of the amydgala was begun by Dr. Joseph LeDoux (1996). *The emotional brain.* New York: Simon and Schuster and is briefly reviewed in Chapter 2 of Goleman's *Emotional intelligence.* The work of Antonio Damasio with human patients is also highly relevant. His book *Descartes' error: Emotion, reason, and the human brain* (1994), New York: Avon Press, contains the essence of his research and his view of the important links between reason and emotion. The roles of the amygdale, thalamus, and hippocampus and the connection between emotion and reason is also nicely spelled out in a web site from McGill University: http://www.thebrain.mcgill.ca/flash/index_d.html

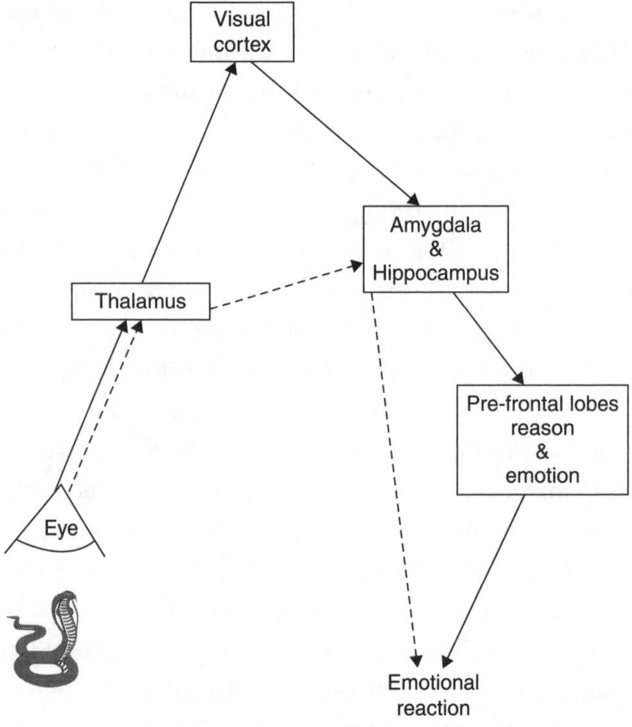

FIGURE 12.2. The Neurology of emotion.
(Solid lines show the normal route. Dashed lines show the emergency route).

the power to initiate immediate action. The amygdala can respond directly, without benefit of higher order thinking. It is a primitive structure but can be life saving as it enables us to act even before knowing why. With the assistance of the hippocampus the amygdala can act even before information is processed by the visual areas of the brain. Thus, we can jump back from the snake even before we consciously see it. There is a kind of thinking going on here, not the rational kind that the Ancient Greeks emphasized, but it is thinking nevertheless. The primitive structures of the limbic system can be rational in their own self-preserving way. They can integrate new, incoming information with old, stored memories to preserve life.

Daniel Goleman describes how fear and anger based on long-forgotten memories or childhood traumas can be stored in the limbic system's components and rise up in the amygdala to produce terrible violence. Goleman tells the story of a man, who was abused as a child and who, upon seeing another person resembling his abusive father, actually killed him. As Goleman relates the tale, upon seeing the father's look-alike, the amygdala took control and caused him to act in a way that reason would have never permitted. Goleman describes this kind of unusual process as "emotional hijacking."

We have all acted on the spur of the moment, "shooting from the hip" and marveled at how and why we behaved as we did. The amygdala operates at a very basic and primitive level. It "thinks" in accord with its past emotional experience and is not in the least bound by the principles of reason. As noted above, it can initiate action even before we are conscious of what we are doing.

Remember William James' elaboration of Darwin's instinct theory of emotion? We act first by instinct and then feel, only after becoming aware of what our bodies are doing. James' view of emotion seems correct under certain emergency circumstances. The old cerebellum part of our brain is meant to protect us. "Instinct," if that is what we want to call it, does have a place in our modern view of emotion.

But action directed by the amygdala is the exception. Typically the presence of the snake would take a longer and more indirect route in the brain. Messages traveling directly from the thalamus to the amygdala, taking the short cut to action, usually occur only in emergency situations. The more likely route is for the visual information to travel from the thalamus to the visual cortex at the rear of the neo-cortex. Here the information is sorted but does not yet constitute a meaningful perception. For that to occur the information must travel through several centers of processing ending up in the prefrontal lobes, the areas of the *cerebral cortex* behind the eyes.

The frontal lobes are the areas of higher level processing, that is, thinking, planning, and forethought. Persons and primates who have suffered damage to their prefrontal areas[2] experience loss of "executive control and self-awareness" resulting in the "loss of foresight, judgment, social graces, creativity, empathy, reasoning and reliability." Here lay the capacities of "executive control," the ability to make reasonable decisions, to inhibit when appropriate, and to say and do the right thing.

The prefrontal lobes appear to be the centers where visual images become meaningful and where reason and emotion join together. The prefrontal lobes, one in the right and one in the left hemisphere of the *cerebral cortex*, may be the seat of our humanness, our *ergon*.

Figure 12.2 shows that emotions generated by the amygdala are normally joined with cognitive activity in the prefrontal lobes. Here feelings and reason come together. Emotional messages from the limbic system combine with the executive functions of the *cerebral cortex*. A snake is spotted in the distance and its markings show it to be just a harmless garden snake. We smile and continue on our way. Reason joining with emotion finds no cause for alarm.

Does all of this sound familiar – the moderation of feeling by reason? Aristotle's *virtue* appears to be consistent with the way the brain works. We have only just begun to understand the physiology of virtue but to this point the evidence fits rather nicely with Aristotle's ideas. We can now talk about the concept of virtue at the philosophical, psychological, and physiological levels.

[2] See Ross, E.D. (1997).Cortical Representation of Emotions in M. Timble & J. Cummings (Eds.), *Behavioural neurology*. Oxford: Butterworth-Heinemann.

13

Emotional Intelligence

> Virtue, according to the utilitarian doctrine, is not naturally and originally part of the end, but is capable of becoming so; and in those who love it disinterestedly it has become so, and is desired and cherished, not as a means to happiness, but as a part of their happiness.
>
> John Stuart Mill (1806–1873) *Utilitarianism, Liberty & Representative Government*

There is another area of contemporary psychology that is supportive of Aristotle's thoughts on virtue. We are familiar with the concepts of intelligence and IQ but there are now counterparts of these ideas in the world of emotion. We can be smart in different ways. Our success in life depends not only on our IQ but also on our emotional intelligence or EI, which has been getting a lot of recognition lately.

The idea of intelligence testing goes at least back to Darwin's cousin, Sir Francis Galton, who developed tests of sensory acuity. Believing that keen senses could take in more of the world and therefore better inform the mind, Galton developed the first psychological tests. Later formulations of intelligence replaced sensory acuity with the ability to reason. Today's IQ tests are variations of those alternatives to Galton's acuity tests.

Epigraph cited in Wenger, M.F. (1991) *An historical introduction to moral philosophy*. Englewood Cliffs, NJ: Prentice Hall, p. 165.

More recently, psychologist Howard Gardener[1] has argued for different kinds of intelligences. He recognizes the traditional linguistic–verbal and logical–mathematical abilities of the standardized intelligence tests but also adds visual–spatial, bodily–kinesthetic, musical–rhythmic, and interpersonal and intrapersonal abilities as well. Just recently Gardener added a naturalist capacity to the list. In any case, we are rapidly moving away from the conventional IQ, which seems to be so important to academic achievement, and toward more specific capacities such as the subject of this chapter, emotional intelligence.

Emotion and reason are usually thought of as separate and even opposing functions. Many still believe that we are at our best when reason overrules untrustworthy feelings. That idea has been passed down for centuries but contemporary cognitive psychology takes a different view. The cognitive approaches of Ellis, Lazarus, Power and Dalgleish, and Epstein, all show how feeling and reason work together, and in the end become inseparable. In the previous chapter we saw how the prefrontal lobes may be the locus of this union.

In the early 1990s, psychologists John Mayer and Peter Salovey[2] introduced the idea of emotional intelligence. The very name brings together feeling and reason. There is presently a flurry of research in the area that has yet to settle down, but I believe emotional intelligence and virtue are very similar ideas.

Mayer and Salovey suggest that emotional intelligence is comprised of four related abilities. First is the ability to *perceive*

[1] Gardner, H. (1983). *Frames of mind: The theory of multiple intelligences*. New York: Basic Books.
(1993). *Multiple intelligences: The theory in practice*. New York: Basic Books.
(1999). *The disciplined mind: What all students should understand*. New York: Simon & Schuster.

[2] Salovey, P., & Mayer, J. D. (1990). Emotional intelligence. *Imagination, Cognition, and Personality*, 9, 185–211. See also, Ciarrochi, J., Forgas, J., & Mayer, J. D. (Eds.) (2001) *Emotional intelligence in everyday life: A scientific inquiry*. Philadelphia PA: Psychology Press.

emotions correctly, both in oneself and in others. We are probably all familiar with someone who has very little insight into his or her own feelings and may also seem oblivious to the feelings of others. Such people are likely to have both personal and social problems. Studies have examined how well people judge emotions from facial expressions and the results show that those who score high on tests of emotional intelligence are better at reading others emotions. It is important to see others accurately if we are to be close to them.

You may remember that Carl Rogers, the humanistic psychologist of the 1960s and 1970s, put a lot of emphasis on what he called "organismic listening" or one's capacity to monitor feelings and desires. People with high emotional intelligence are just more attuned and more accurate in their perceptions of feelings, both in themselves and in others. To the degree that this ability is present, a person will guide his or her actions, especially toward others, in more effective and satisfactory ways.

Second, we find that because people with high emotional intelligence are better at reading emotion, they are able to use them to *enhance their thinking and decision making.* As noted above, we often pit reason and emotion one against the other. But, if you think about it, you will find yourself using feelings to make decisions all the time. "How do you feel about it" is a commonly used phrase. "Go with your guts" is a similar idea. As we suggested earlier, not all thinking is truly conscious and rational. Sometimes we just "feel it in our bones" or "know it in our hearts." People with high emotional intelligence trust their feelings and use them adaptively. In the real world there may be no such thing as "pure reason." Our thoughts and decisions are often colored by our feelings, which appears to be a good thing.

The third component of Mayer and Salovey's emotional intelligence is the ability to *understand emotions and their meanings.* Knowledge about emotion is essential to successful living. We must understand the causes of emotions and how they affect behavior.

We have to know what kinds of actions make others angry. If a wife does not understand that her flirting makes her husband angry and jealous, she is not likely to stay married. If a person constantly gossips at work, his relationships with co-workers will soon deteriorate. To be effective we have to know what it feels like to be ashamed or embarrassed or humiliated. We have to know what causes these emotions and we must know how to react to them. An understanding of emotions in general is an essential ingredient of emotional intelligence.

The fourth component of emotional intelligence identified by Mayer and Salovey is the *ability to manage emotion* both in the self and in others. This seems to be what most of us think of when we consider the influence of reason on emotion. It refers to the ability to control our own feelings and to adjust them according to circumstances. But it also includes the ability to respond appropriately to the emotional behavior of others. Of course, we must be able to control our anger and expression of displeasure or disappointment. Remember that little book of a few years ago, "Don't Sweat the Small Stuff"? The author has a point. "There is a time" for all emotions but we must choose correctly as we manage them. This is the thesis of Aristotle's *Ethics* and the function of virtue. Thinking back to Chapter 11 where we considered the different ways to alter emotion by reappraisal, behavioral coping, and developing automatic or habitual modes of coping, we see that emotional management has been a central idea in psychology for a long time. Managing emotions is critical to living with our selves and with others.

In 1995 Daniel Goleman popularized the idea of emotional intelligence in his best selling book by that name.[3] Goleman identifies five components of emotional intelligence that are just slightly different than those identified by Mayer and Salovey. In a *Harvard*

[3] Goleman, D. (1995). *Emotional intelligence.* New York: Bantam Books. Also see Goleman, D. (1998). What makes a good leader. *Harvard Business Review,* Nov./Dec.

Business Review article where he applies emotional intelligence to work settings, Goleman refers to: (1) self-awareness, the ability to recognize and understand one's own emotions; (2) self-regulation, the ability to control disruptive impulses; (3) motivation, the passion for the tasks we do; (4) empathy, the ability to understand others emotions; and (5) social skill, managing relationships with others.

In a later book entitled *Working with Emotional Intelligence,*[4] Goleman suggested that emotional intelligence is an overarching ability or capacity to bring together emotion and cognition in these five areas, but a person must also develop certain *emotional competencies* in each area. Emotional competencies are *learned*, so that one can work on and develop the necessary skills for a good life and a successful career. Goleman has devoted his latest efforts to developing competencies in the professional world of executives and managers. He claims that emotional intelligence and competence is much more important to success than IQ or technical knowledge, especially at the higher levels of the business world. "Compared to IQ and expertise, emotional competence mattered *twice* as much. This held across all categories of jobs, and in all kinds of organizations."

Israeli psychologist Reuven Bar-On[5] has offered a slightly modified model of emotional intelligence that includes components similar to the ones identified by Goleman and by Mayer and Salovey and adds a few others as well. Most interesting to us is the finding that when Bar-On studied the relationship between emotional intelligence and self-actualization, the correlation was extremely high. His results suggest that 60 percent of self-actualization can be explained by emotional intelligence and only 40 percent by the combined influence of cognitive intelligence, education, and experience. This

[4] Goleman, D. (1999). *Working with emotional intelligence.* New York: Bantam Books. See page 31 for the importance of EQ compared to IQ.

[5] Bar-On, R. (2001). Emotional intelligence and self-actualization. In J. Ciarrochi, J. Forgas, & J. D. Mayer (Eds.) *Emotional intelligence in everyday life: A scientific inquiry.* New York: Psychology Press.

finding is really quite remarkable and has now been replicated in several studies. Bar-On suggests that "emotional-social intelligence much more than cognitive intelligence … influences one's ability to do one's best, to accomplish goals and to actualize one's potential to the fullest."[6] If, as Aristotle and the Humanistic psychologists claim, fulfillment and actualization *are* happiness, and if, as it appears, emotional intelligence is a refinement of Aristotle's concept of virtue, then we have very strong evidence for the view presented here. Clearly, more research on the relationship between emotional intelligence and well-being is needed, but Bar-On's findings are very encouraging.

Emotional intelligence is both intrapersonal and interpersonal. Goleman gives about equal weight to personal competence and social competence. Everyone recognizes the importance of social skills for a good life and some psychologists have focused on *social intelligence* as a different kind of noncognitive intelligence, but at this point it is unclear if still another kind of intelligence is necessary. Finally, Sternberg[7] and others have studied the qualities of emotional and social intelligence together, along with other abilities, to form an inclusive category they call *practical intelligence.* Practical intelligence is used to solve everyday life problems like the choice of a career or mate, or how to help a friend in trouble, or plan a route to a distant place. Some think that emotional intelligence is too restrictive

[6] Bar-On, R. (2006) The Bar-On model of social and emotional intelligence (ESI) (1). *Psicothema, 18*, suppl., 13–25. Can be found at http://www.eiconsortium.org/reprints/bar-on_model_of_Emotional-social_intelligence.htm

[7] Hedlund, J., & Sternberg, R. J. (2000). Too many intelligences? Integrating social, emotional and practical intelligence. In R. Bar-On & J. D. Parker (Eds.), *The handbook of emotional intelligence: Theory, development, assessment and application at home, school, and in the work place.* San Francisco: Jossey-Bass. See also Sternberg, R. J. (2001). Measuring the intelligence of an idea: how intelligent is the idea of emotional intelligence? In J. Ciarrochi, J. P. Forgas, & J. D. Mayer (Eds.), *Emotional intelligence in everyday life: A scientific inquiry.* New York: Psychological Press.

and that the ability to solve problems, whether emotional, social, or task centered, may depend on a single general ability.

The research in these areas is moving at a fast clip and it is still difficult to know where the findings will lead and which ideas will endure. However, one thing is clear. *Emotional intelligence*, however it is conceived, is strikingly supportive of Aristotle's ideas on virtue. The integration of feeling with thinking and behavior is the central idea in all of the views we have covered here. Let me refer once again to Aristotle's seminal thought:

> The mean and the good is feeling at the right time, about the right things in relation to the right people and for the right reason; and the mean and the good are the task of virtue. Similarly, in regard to actions there are excess, deficiency, and the mean.

Aristotle didn't break it down into emotional, personal, social, or practical intelligence but he had the right idea. Virtue now goes by many names but the *golden mean* is still the center of the target and emotion melded with reason is still essential to an accurate arrow.

14

The Development of Virtue

> It makes no small difference, then, whether we form habits of one kind or of another from our very youth; it makes a very great difference, or rather *all* the difference.
>
> Aristotle, *Nicomachaen Ethics*, Book II Chapter 1.

In 1924, after John B. Watson declared that Behaviorism could train any child to become a "doctor, lawyer, artist, merchant-chief and, yes, even beggar-man and thief," he added the following qualification: "please note that when this experiment is made I am to be allowed to specify the way the children are to be *brought up* and the type of world they have to live in."[1]

Watson admitted that he was exaggerating but was trying to make a point: The world we live in is critical to our development and the early years are especially important. Although Aristotle would have been appalled by Watson's methods of child rearing, he would have agreed about the importance of the environment and the early years. For Aristotle a good life requires virtue and childhood is where virtue begins.

Remember, virtue includes *desire*, *thinking*, *feeling*, and *action* (see Figure 9.1). For each of us there is an optimal response to every situation. We might respond differently yet correctly. Because "right action" depends on individual differences and circumstances,

[1] Watson, J. B. (1970/1924). *Behaviorism*. New York: W.W. Norton & Co. Inc., Chapter V, p. 104.

teaching specific correct behaviors is almost impossible. How could we ever anticipate every situation and take into account our manifold differences as well? The possibilities are endless. Virtue can not be reduced to a set of behaviors or even rules. The best that we can do is prepare a child to choose wisely. Aristotle had some pretty insightful thoughts on how this might be accomplished.

Let us agree at the outset that children are not little adults. A virtuous person analyzes a situation, wants to do the right thing and enjoys doing it. True virtue requires understanding of situations, mature desire, moderated feelings, and guided action. Such complex processes cannot be expected of children. What we can and should do, however, is teach children to behave properly in the situations they face. Kids must learn by doing and from their actions understanding may follow, gradually and slowly. Some of my grandchildren do not yet fully understand the meaning of temperance or the limitations of pleasure, but they can and do frequently act temperately. When Henry pleaded that he "needed" a particular toy we politely explained to him that he will have to wait a few days. He waited. When Lydia wanted another candy bar, her mother said that she had had enough for today. She accepted the admonition and went on with her playing. Henry and Lydia acted appropriately even though they did not truly understand.

Aristotle tells us that the carpenter learns by building, the violinist by playing his instrument, the teacher by teaching. We all learn by doing but it is especially important for children. "It makes no small difference, then, whether we form habits of one kind or of another from our very youth; it makes a very great difference, or rather *all* the difference."[2]

A child may not be able to comprehend the reasons for acting temperately or courageously or fairly, but he can nevertheless perform such behaviors. We can encourage a child to share his toys

[2] Aristotle. *Nichomachean Ethics*, Book II, Chapter 1.

and be strong when he is at the doctor's office. We can let him know that there are limits to what he can buy when accompanying his parents to the store. We can offer direction, words of praise and rewards for proper behavior. And, initially these parental guides are sufficient to sustain appropriate behavior. Rewards and punishments can be necessary and effective determinants of action. But, over time, as Aristotle saw it, something different gradually develops. Virtue and character emerge from these roots.

Let's return again to learning to ride a bicycle. Do you remember that as you gradually developed the right set of habits, the experience became very rewarding in itself? Perhaps praise and pushes and shouts to pedal harder helped at first, but once the thrill of riding began to develop, no outside forces were needed. The action itself was the reward. Psychologists call that intrinsic motivation. The desire to act comes from within. Like all kids, our grandchildren demonstrate intrinsic motivation every day. Audrey loves to write stories and do craft projects but talking on the telephone with friends now seem to be taking precedence. Henry enjoys drawing so much he wants an art lesson every day. His sister Lydia loves riding horses and playing the piano. Noah can't get enough of dinosaurs and video games. Hannah now loves kindergarten more than weekends and loves playing with her friends next door. Jack, nimble and athletic, never stops moving. Writing, creating, playing, growing are the goals here. Potentials in search of fulfillment provide the energy and direction for behavior. Extrinsic rewards seem unimportant to so much of what we do.

As children play, as the builder builds, and as the tennis player swings, skills strengthen, projects take shape, and games are enjoyed; these are reward enough. Doing brings pleasure. *But doing also brings understanding.* You can know that riding a bike is good but until you have ridden yourself, you don't really understand it. I "know" that parenting is hard work; Brenda explained it to me for years. But I really did not understand until we began to baby sit our grandchildren. For most of my adult life I was devoted to my work and pretty much left the childrearing to Brenda, who was much better at it than I. But when we became grandparents and I watched my children and their spouses care for their own children I was amazed at how much time, effort, and energy was required. As Brenda and I babysat our grandchildren it began to sink in just how demanding a job it is. Only when I fully participated in the task did I come to understand the rigors of child care. Earlier I "knew" but I didn't understand.

And so it is with virtue. As a child develops a habit, a *hexis*, she gradually comes to understand her actions and why they are good. She comes to enjoy being fair, being a good friend, and being courageous. She gradually comes to understand her behavior and slowly replaces extrinsic reward with intrinsic motivation. Virtue becomes its own reward. She derives pleasure from doing the right thing and she understands her actions in a way that was not possible when the actions were habitual and externally directed.

Reward, habit, advice, and direction, these are the starting places. But over time habit gives way to understanding and to intrinsic motivation. As a child learns to play an instrument, say the piano, she is first guided by the parent and teacher and the notes and the rules of practice. But something changes over time. Often or at least some of the time, the child begins to understand music – the notes and timing and intensity, the feeling of the melody. She begins to enjoy the activity itself and no longer needs the external rewards, threats, or praise that once kept her sitting at the keyboard. Habit can turn to love. Making music with feeling, desire, and understanding has replaced the earlier mechanical motions.

There is another important effect of practice. As understanding grows, so do perceptual abilities. We talked earlier about *practical wisdom*, that part of intellectual virtue so essential to moral virtue. *Practical wisdom* refers to the capacity to assess and evaluate circumstances and find appropriate actions. For Aristotle, practice plays a role here as well. The understanding that grows with practice and repetition is accompanied by greater and greater powers to discriminate among and within situations.[3] Rote habits gradually turn into cognitively controlled activities where reason, consciousness, and discrimination powers come to govern behavior.

Eventually we are good at knowing which action goes with which circumstance. We know when to be honest and when not to be. We know to tell our host that the party was enjoyable even if we had a terrible time. That is, we learn to discriminate among situations and to select the appropriate response for each. Virtue is developing.

Aristotle's ideas about virtue development are not terribly specific or complete. We might summarize them very simply: Children don't think like adults and if encouraged to act appropriately, they will gradually come to understand their actions and develop intrinsic motivation to perform them. Psychology did not exist 2,500 years ago but the principles outlined by Aristotle seem to be sound and supported by recent psychological theory and research that will be the focus of our next chapter.

[3] I am grateful to Nancy Sherman for this idea found in her article "The Habituation of Character," Chapter 10, in *Aristotle's Ethics: Critical Essays.* (1999). N. Sherman Ed., Lanham, MD: Rowman & Littlefield Publishers.

15

Psychological Views of Virtue Development

> All would agree that the legislator should make education of the young his chief and foremost concern.
>
> Aristotle, *Politics* Book VIII, Chapter 1

Having reviewed Aristotle's thoughts on the development of virtue we will now take a look at some contemporary psychological thinking on the subject. When psychology became an empirical science in the late nineteenth century, concepts like virtue and character went largely unnoticed because they could not be examined in the laboratory. Even today the suspicion of philosophical concepts endures in psychology. However, things are changing. Peterson and Seligman[1] have produced a scholarly and impressively comprehensive handbook on the subjects of character and virtue. Rather than avoiding the philosophical literature they have embraced portions of it to set the stage for a psychological analysis of what they deem the major virtues and noting that they are desperately needed to redirect our society. "After a detour through the hedonism of the 1960s, the narcissism of the 1970s, the materialism of the 1980s, and the apathy of the 1990s, most everyone today seems to believe that character is

[1] Peterson C., & Seligman M. E. P. (2004). *Character strengths and virtues: A handbook and classification*. New York: Oxford University Press. Their discussion of the virtues, many similar to those identified by Aristotle, is excellent. However, the conceptual ties and common theoretical underpinnings identified in Aristotle's treatment of virtue is not apparent.

important after all." Peterson and Seligman do a wonderful job of describing certain core virtues that seem to transcend culture. The theory and evidence they review includes what psychologists have for many years referred to as *moral development.* The psychological study of moral development addresses many of the issues raised by Aristotle, including the limited cognitive abilities of young children and the need for careful guidance during this period. Reason is the very core of virtue but as we know, the ability to reason well develops slowly and gradually.

PIAGET ON MORAL DEVELOPMENT

Jean Piaget, a Swiss biologist turned psychologist, was among the first to empirically study how children reason and included moral reasoning in his studies.[2] Piaget used the concept of *schema* to describe our mental structures. The *schemata* (plural of schema) of the newborn are very primitive and unorganized, consisting largely of mechanisms for reflexes like sucking and grasping. Piaget calls the first stage of cognitive development the *sensorimotor stage* to underscore its reflexive nature. At about two years of age the child enters the *preoperational stage* and begins to form mental images and structures that stand for things in the world. Logical thinking is not yet in the picture; it comes in the next stage called the *concrete operational stage.* Between the ages of about seven and eleven years, children begin to understand the connections between things but are not yet able to grasp abstract ideas. For example, rules are taken as concrete truths that must be followed. Similarly, authority is accepted as absolute and must be obeyed. Thus, "good" is that which is in accord with rules and authority; "good" is not yet an abstract idea. By the age of twelve or so, the child enters the stage of *formal operations.* Now ideas

[2] Piaget, J. (1932/1965). *The moral judgment of the child.* New York: Basic Books.

like goodness and fairness begin to develop so that the child can evaluate actions and rules by comparing them to these ideas. True understanding is beginning to emerge. The child is now able to make judgments about goodness and fairness in a general way and over a range of situations.

Progress through these cognitive stages is not necessarily automatic or biologically determined. Piaget points to the importance of adults and other children because it is through encounters with them that absolute rules come into question. As a victim of unfair practices the child may come to realize and understand the injustice of something he readily accepted at an earlier time. As the child plays with others he may struggle to clarify his ideas about fairness and courage. Able to envision the future, he can now appreciate the benefits of temperance and friendship. He can accept delay of reward because he understands that something better will happen shortly. He can be kind to his playmate because he knows it will be reciprocated. He is beginning to develop ideas that can be used as standards to evaluate a wide range of actions.

Piaget opposed teaching rules about right and wrong and good and bad, but preferred allowing the child, *when ready*, to develop them herself through experience. In the early stages of cognitive development, the child needs rules and guidance, but later, in the periods of concrete and formal operations, the child must *learn by doing*; just as Aristotle suggested. Young children need rules because they cannot understand abstract ideas. As they mature ideas are developed *by doing*. Parents contribute greatly to both periods; the early stages require authority and rules, and the later stages require explanation in a form that the child can understand. Parents must allow children to discover things for themselves. Through willful action a child can test his emerging moral principles. Peers and siblings are also essential to moral education. It is through interaction and sometimes conflict with them that a child comes to truly understand what is right and what is wrong. Aristotle probably would have liked Piaget's thinking: rote, rules, and obedience at first, then gradual development of understanding.

KOHLBERG ON MORAL DEVELOPMENT

Lawrence Kohlberg, a Harvard psychologist, carried Piaget's theory of moral development beyond childhood and into adulthood.[3] Like Piaget, Kohlberg studied how people think as they solve moral problems. Again, we find age-related differences in thinking about right and wrong but, according to Kohlberg, age is no guarantee of virtue development.

Kohlberg describes moral development as proceeding in six stages, divided into three levels. These are summarized below.

Level I: Preconventional Morality

Stage 1: Reward and Punishment Orientation

At this stage acts are judged according to their consequences. An act is good if it is rewarded and bad if it is punished. Right and wrong are determined by outcome, not by abstract principle or reasoning.

Stage 2: Instrumental Orientation

At this stage the person has developed a future orientation and can foresee consequences. The ideas of fairness and sharing begin to develop, not because these are right or just, but because they are useful. "If I am nice to you, then you will be nice to me." Reciprocity is present but it is still viewed in terms of consequences, not as a moral principle. This stage is sometimes described as "you scratch my back and I'll scratch yours." Outcome is central, not idea. Reasoning is still pretty primitive.

[3] Kohlberg, L. (1976). Moral stages and moralization. In T. Lickona (Ed.), *Handbook of socialization theory* (pp. 31–53). New York: Holt, Rinehart & Winston.

Level II: Conventional Level

Stage 3: Good Boy/Nice Girl

At this stage people tend to judge good and bad and right and wrong according to social conventions. It is the family, the peer group, or the nation that defines what is acceptable and what is not. An action is good if others say it is. Once again, reasoning is only poorly developed and similar to Piaget's concrete operational stage.

Stage 4: "Law and Order Orientation"

Also in the concrete operational stage these people tend to agree with authority and rules. Maintenance of the social order is most important and right is doing one's duty by obeying the rules.

Level III: Postconventional Or Principled Orientation

Stage 5: Social Contract Orientation

At this level people tend to be guided by ideas or principles rather than social groups or rules. The principles embraced tend to support the rights of individuals as well as the social order. This stage is sometimes referred to as the "legalistic orientation" because it recognizes the legal rights of every individual. It is a utilitarian view and what works for the individual is favored and considered good and just.

Stage 6: Universal Ethical Principles

Kohlberg believed that regardless of culture or accepted social conventions, some (a few) people will choose to follow certain ethical principles like the golden rule, justice, and the sanctity of life. Such people are considered to have attained a highly developed sense of morality and are not bound by utility or social pressures but rather have chosen to follow their own, self-selected and reasoned principles. Kohlberg believed that highly moral individuals would agree on what is good and bad despite differences in culture because their guiding principles are derived from the same universal truths available to everyone but embraced by only a few.

Kohlberg's theory can be very useful for understanding why people make the moral decisions they do. From his point of view we all decide about right and wrong but we do it differently. Some judge an act by its consequences, some by its social acceptance, and the more advanced tend to use universally accepted moral principles. We are all moral philosophers but because we reason differently we use different criteria to make moral decisions.[4]

For Kohlberg, as for Piaget, it is not so much an action but rather the thinking behind it that determines its morality. We might do something good for the wrong reason or something bad for the right reason. Charitable giving for tax purposes might not be an act of kindness at all, while giving to a corrupt charity might be done with the best of intentions. It is the thinking behind the act that determines its goodness.

The ideas of Piaget and Kohlberg are consistent with Aristotle's view of virtue development but they are clearly more advanced. We have a much better understanding of cognitive development than we did 2,500 years ago and can see more clearly why children are so dependent upon sound adult guidance and the opportunity for willful action, the chance to "do" and therefore to understand. Remember, virtue boils down to the moderation of emotion by reason. While Piaget and Kohlberg have focused primarily on the reasoning part, others have concentrated on the development of emotion.

[4] Gilligan, C. (1982). *In a different voice: Psychological theory and women's development. Cambridge: Harvard University Press.* A student of Kohlberg, Gilligan proposed a variation of his theory. She suggests that Kohlberg's studies, which used male subjects, were not representative of women's moral thinking. She observes that women's moral judgments are likely to consider the welfare of others and personal caring more than the rational principles identified by Kohlberg. Some research suggests that both abstract principle and caring may be bases of moral reasoning but the role of personal caring needs more research.

THE EMOTIONAL BASICS

Daniel Goleman reminds us that emotional learning begins at birth.[5] Back in the 1950s psychologist Erik Erickson suggested that the first year of life is mainly about the development of trust. If a parent or caretaker fulfills the needs of a child, the child learns that the world is a safe and trustworthy place. If the child's needs are not met, the child learns to mistrust. The world can be viewed as a safe or as a dangerous place and these emotional expectations develop from the very beginning. The family can be a source of security or insecurity; of comfort or fear.

Goleman points out that if parents are to provide the basics of emotional learning to a child they themselves must be pretty well grounded emotionally. Emotional learning happens in just about every interaction with parents. If parents demonstrate caring, empathy, and understanding the child will probably know emotional well-being, but if the child's early experience is saturated with unhealthy and damaging emotions, the child will most likely carry those feelings to other relationships as life progresses.

Psychologists Elias, Tobias, and Friedlander[6] used Goleman's ideas about emotional intelligence to write a book for parents on how to raise emotionally intelligent children. They point out that feelings convey a lot of information. Feeling bad usually means that something is wrong and feeling good often means that we are doing something right.[7] In either case *emotional awareness* can be a first step to emotionally intelligent behavior.

[5] Goleman, D. (1995). *Emotional intelligence* New York: Bantam Books.

[6] Elias, M., Tobias, S., & Freidlander, B. (1999). *Emotionally intelligent parenting. How to raise a self-disciplined, responsible, socially skilled child.* New York: Random House.

[7] See Klinger, E. (1977). *Meaning and void: Inner experience and the incentives in people's lives.* Minneapolis: University of Minnesota Press. Klinger was one of the first to discuss the role of emotion as a guide to action.

Feeling bad doesn't really solve anything but learning to control such feelings can be very helpful. Elias and his colleagues advise parents to guide their children in *learning how to change feelings*. Whether it is anger, disappointment, or sadness, a child can come to understand that feelings are changeable. This may involve learning how to set goals and sub-goals and to solve problems. Of course, instruction must be framed in terms that a child can understand, but when correctly carried out, the child can learn *self-control*, to manage feelings, desire, and actions. He can learn to seek *the golden mean*.

Remember Aristotle's *practical wisdom* and its importance to all the virtues. *Practical wisdom* is an intellectual virtue but guides moral virtues like courage and temperance by analyzing circumstances and selecting a correct response for the occasion. *Practical wisdom* requires attention to situational detail and the ability to make perceptual discriminations between situations. These perceptual and cognitive abilities come slowly and are age related. In her book on self-control, Alexandra Logue[8] discusses some of the cognitive abilities that impact self-control and their relation to age. To attend to the critical dimensions of a situation, to select an appropriate action, and to judge future consequences require considerable brain power that takes years to develop.[9] We cannot expect too much from children and we must help them cultivate these abilities so that they can know happiness in the years ahead.

Soon after the publication of Goleman's *Emotional Intelligence*, psychologist John Gottman published a book entitled *The Heart of*

[8] Logue, A.W. (1995). *Self-control: Waiting until tomorrow for what you want today*. Englewood Cliffs, NJ: Prentice Hall.

[9] Recent research suggests that different virtues may develop at different ages. See for example, Park, N. and Peterson, C. (2006). Character strengths and happiness among young children: Content analysis of parental descriptions. *Journal of Happiness Studies*, *7*, 323–341.

Parenting: How to Raise an Emotionally Intelligent Child.[10] Gottman points out that we should be aware that some emotional intelligence is determined by built-in genetic causes, but the influence of experience with parents is still a very important factor in a child's emotional life. He identifies five key steps that parents can take to raise an emotionally healthy child.

Empathy for the child is the foundation upon which all of the five steps rest. Empathy is simply feeling what another person is feeling. Gottman has found that empathy is not only a feeling but includes physical responses, too. When an empathic person observes another's emotions she will experience similar *feelings and bodily responses.* When a child is hurting, afraid, or angry, a capable parent can, to some degree, get inside that child to feel what the child feels both psychologically and physically. That ability has very important consequences. "Empathy allows children to see their parents as allies."

Children believe parents and adults are smart and are usually right about things. So, when the parent communicates understanding of how a child feels, the child's emotions are validated – his parent feels the same way, so his emotion must be okay. Perceiving this similarity, the child builds trust in his own emotions as well as intimacy with the parent. If the parent effectively deals with the emotion, the child can observe and model this behavior to strengthen his own emotional intelligence.

Let me briefly illustrate empathy with a true story about my grandson and his mother. Noah became very upset when told to turn off a video game. He cried softly and was very frustrated, even angry. His mother gathered Noah in her arms and softly explained that she understood his frustration and knew that stopping a video game in the middle is hard to do. She explained further, in a soothing voice, that if he calmed down he would soon be able to go back to the game

[10] Gottman, J. (1997). *The heart of parenting: How to raise an emotionally intelligent child.* New York: Simon & Schuster.

when we (the grandparents) left for the hotel. It took a couple of minutes but Noah calmed himself and rejoined the family. His mother did an excellent job of showing Noah affection while empathizing with his frustration. By remaining calm throughout the episode she enabled Noah to observe and to copy her emotional response.

Here are Gottman's five steps to building empathy and emotional intelligence in children.

1. *Be aware of a child's emotions.* First, a parent or caretaker must attend to the child's feelings. In order to do that, the parent must be able to recognize emotion in him- or herself. We differ in our abilities to express emotion but we all feel and we all benefit from "listening" to those feelings. If I can acknowledge my own anger, sadness, anxiety, and so on, I will be able to see it in others. Children may not express their feelings the same way we adults do, but an attentive parent may be able to see emotion expressed in the child's play, interaction with other children, nightmares, or stomach aches. And, when your heart goes out to a child, you are experiencing empathy. Now you have the chance to build trust and offer guidance, to build the child's emotional intelligence.
2. *Recognize emotion as a chance for intimacy and teaching.* Gottman says "By acknowledging our children's emotions, we are helping them learn skills for soothing themselves, skills that will serve them well for a lifetime." Negative feelings usually decrease when children talk about them. When parents try to ignore or even make fun of a child's anger or fear or sadness, those emotions usually get stronger. But when the child feels that his discomfort is recognized and attended to, the emotion subsides and, as it does, the bond between the parent and child grows stronger.
3. *Validate the child's feelings.* When a child feels bad about something many of us try to solve the problem. "Oh, Jenny

really does like you despite her meanness to you today." "Don't worry you'll get a good grade on the next test." Or "Daddy can take you to the playground even though the other kids left you out." Kids don't really want solutions when they are feeling bad, they want understanding and validation of their reaction. Just listening – serious, attentive, empathetic understanding – is what the child needs first. Once she believes that you, the wise and all-knowing adult, understands and appreciates her feelings, then she might be open to problem solving.

4. *Help with labeling emotion.* If a child is to develop a high level of emotional intelligence he has to be able to discriminate between feelings. Emotional arousal can be very confusing; fear, anger, sadness and any of a score of different feelings can descend upon us, and then there are the countless mixed emotions that we have to cope with. To learn the labels of different feelings and to understand the causes of each can help a child develop a vocabulary that may assist him in understanding and coping with emotion.
5. *Help with problem solving.* To tell a child to stop crying or stop being so angry is not terribly helpful; feelings don't go away because we tell them to. Telling a child what she *ought* to feel makes her distrust what she *does* feel and "leads to self-doubt and loss of self-esteem." A better way to change emotion is to work on the problem that produced the emotion but Gottman reminds us that kids are usually not very good problem solvers. They think concretely and find it hard to imagine different possibilities. Six-year-old Alex may not be able to think of a way to stop his sister from teasing him. A parent can help, though, by asking Alex what might make *him* stop teasing someone or by offering suggestions that he might consider. Gottman points out, however, that "if you really want your child to own the outcome, you should encourage her to generate her own ideas." So, rather than suggesting a solution it is

> best to encourage and assist the child in generating a solution of her own.

To summarize Gottman's method of developing emotional intelligence we should first be aware of a child's emotions. This awareness helps to establish intimacy between adult and child. It will also help the child to understand emotion and its causes, and validate his feelings. Because emotions can be vague, complex, and confusing, helping a child to label feelings may assist him in dealing with them. Finally, the adult should help the child to find solutions for controlling and changing feelings, so that he may react with emotional intelligence in the future.

While Gottman's advice is much more detailed than the guidance offered by Aristotle, the two are quite compatible. Recall that Aristotle first urges us to direct the behavior and then, gradually, help the child understand and control the behavior. Gottman's five steps can help guide us through the second stage.

DEVELOPING VIRTUE IN SCHOOLS

Moral education is important to most of us but in the early twentieth century American education consciously turned away from character development and devoted itself to the generation and dissemination of information. Universities increasingly accepted the task of research and placed student development in a distant second position. In the 1960s American educational institutions actually embraced a morally neutral philosophy. The growth of relativism and the emphasis on individualism overshadowed what little remained of concern for values and virtues. Values were considered to be an individual matter and it was improper to impose ones view upon another. Tolerance of others, to the point of indiscriminate acceptance, was the watchword. The possibility of universal ideals common to all was suspect if not flatly rejected. "You have your truth and I have mine" was a popular slogan.

In recent years, however, we have witnessed a renewed interest in character education. Kohlberg's elaboration of Piaget's ideas opened a door that had been closed for many years. Noddings[11] observes that "People want to be happy and, since this desire is well-nigh universal, we would expect to find happiness included as an aim of education." She further notes that to do this "schools should show the society that a democracy honors all of its honest workers, not just those who finish college and make a lot of money." Few today would argue against including instruction on personal development in some form in public institutions. Not only are parents responsible for their children, we as members of a society share in that obligation. The development of children as persons and as responsible adults is everybody's business. We are, in some ways, returning to Aristotle's view.

Concerned with the governance of the Greek city-states, Aristotle's *Politics*[12] followed the *Nichomachaen Ethics*. The final chapter, Book VIII, of the *Politics* is entitled "Training of Youth." Recognizing that youth are the future of any society Aristotle suggests that education should *not* be left to parents alone but should be the responsibility of the entire community. The first sentence of Book VIII reads "All would agree that the legislator should make education of the young his chief and foremost concern." The welfare and very survival of a community ultimately rests upon the foundation of virtues passed to its children.

In Aristotle's time Athens was both city and nation (called a city-state) and had a population of only about 200,000. It is difficult to compare such a community with many of today's giant and

[11] Noddings, N. (2003). *Happiness and education*. Cambridge, UK: Cambridge University Press. See especially pp. 74 and 86.

[12] Aristotle. (1952). *Politics*. In the *Great Books of the Western World*, R. M. Hutchins & M. J. Adler (Eds.) Chicago: Encyclopedia Britannica.

diverse cities where the influences on youth are far more complex. Television, music, and the media in general are now powerful forces in the lives of children. Peer influence is a terribly powerful determinant of values and behavior. Many of these forces are difficult to control and passing the virtues that we may wish for our children is not without difficulty. Yet, Aristotle's ideas about politics may still be relevant. Character education and virtue are in fact returning to public education. There is still disagreement about how best to build character in our youth but many of the contemporary approaches resemble Aristotle's ancient formula.

Huitt[13] discusses several approaches that are under consideration today. Some communities believe that character education should be left entirely in the hands of parents and *out of the public domain*. Others believe the *values clarification* approach is the correct way to go, a view which holds that virtues are culturally specific and that no culture has better values than another, they are only different. Aristotle, of course, would disagree. He would probably suggest that we are all human beings and, therefore, by nature have quite similar needs. That's why fairness, friendship, and courage are almost universally recognized as virtues.[14]

Third, there is the *cognitive approach*, which holds that moral decisions are made rationally and that rational discussion is the best way to develop virtues. This is the position taken by both Piaget and Kohlberg, however they recognize that discussion need not always involve teachers or parents. Children are often forced to think about moral issues when they interact with siblings and peers. As mentioned earlier, a child who suffers mistreatment at the hands of friends or brothers and sisters may very well be inclined to think about fairness and injustice. Of course, children also learn from

[13] Huitt, W. (2004). *Moral and character development.* Educational Psychology Interactive. Valdosta, GA: Valdosta State University. Retrieved November 2, 2005, from http://Chiron.valdosta.edu/whuitt/col.morchr.html.

[14] See Peterson and Seligman, pp. 51–52.

parents, teachers, and other adults by observing their reactions to transgressions of acceptable behavior and thus providing moral instruction. Parents and teachers must, however, keep the cognitive development of the child in mind and present ideas at a level that the child can understand.

Huitt also presents what he calls the *inculcation* approach to moral education. Here a set of values is selected and taught as though they are universally agreed upon and appropriate to all situations. Some religious education may include this view of virtue and morality. Finally, there is the *action learning perspective*, which stresses the importance of putting into action the cognitive ideals that have been learned.

Huitt incorporates several of these approaches into what he calls the *systems view*. This position seems especially consistent with Aristotle's ideas about the development of virtue by first learning to act morally and then gradually coming to understand why. Huitt suggests that students first develop a knowledge base of right and wrong and good and bad. Certain behaviors are acceptable and others are not. Some of this knowledge base becomes valued and valued ideas become guides for behavior. For example, a child may learn that cooperation with other children is praiseworthy. As he comes to value that idea, he may use it in his interaction with others. Then, according to Huitt, "as students reflect on their behavior, it adds to the knowledge base, strengthens their thinking skills, and (further) impacts their values."

Thus, as Aristotle suggested, children act and only later come to understand their actions in a morally significant way. Huitt puts it so: "As important as it is to impact overt behavior, it is equally important to help students make explicit [their] own knowledge base, value system … so as to make that behavior more intentional."

Although character education is much more complicated than he outlined, Aristotle's basic idea about virtuous behavior preceding understanding seems to have survived and to have been adopted by many at the forefront of today's educational establishment.

EMOTIONAL INTELLIGENCE IN EDUCATION

The idea of emotional intelligence has begun to enter public education as well as the home and office. Many believe that instruction in emotional intelligence should be included in the curriculum from kindergarten through high school. Daniel Goleman and Eileen Rockefeller Growald have developed a foundation to promote and establish *social emotional learning* (SEL) programs throughout the country and even worldwide. Their foundation *The Collaborative to Advance Social and Emotional Learning* (CASEL) is devoted to creating a network of interested scientists, educators and policymakers, for the purpose of advancing the cause of SEL.[15]

Elias, Hunter, and Kress[16] have reviewed several programs currently in progress. This is not the place to discuss the details of these programs but in one way or another they are all concerned with identifying, understanding, and regulating emotions. Programs also include instruction in problem solving, interpersonal relations, self-calming exercises, and so on. Some programs attempt to develop communities within the school environment where students can actually practice the skills they are learning. In seems that it has once again become fashionable, or perhaps even essential, to educate our youth in virtue. Aristotle would certainly approve. Remember, "it makes no small difference, it makes all the difference."

[15] The Goleman/Rockefeller Growald SEL website is www.CASEL.org

[16] Elias, M. J., Hunter, L., & Kress, J.S. (2001). Emotional intelligence and education. In J. Ciarrochi, J. Forgas, & J. D. Mayer (Eds.) *Emotional intelligence in everyday life: Aa scientific inquiry.* New York:. Psychology Press.

16

The Polis

> To establish justice, insure domestic tranquility, provide for the common defense, promote the general welfare, and secure the blessings of liberty.
>
> *The Constitution of the United States of America*

The parents, teachers, and friends who are responsible for virtue development in children are part of a larger community that Aristotle called the *polis*. The *polis* is necessary for our well-being and even for our very survival. It is only in the *polis* that we can obtain the goods we need to actualize potentials. We need food from the grocery store, books from the library, heat from the utility company, and police protection from those who would harm us. Of course, we can obtain some goods ourselves, alone in the wilderness, but the fact that almost all of us choose to live among others testifies to the need for the *polis*. Yes, it is common to want to be away and free from the maddening crowd for a short time but we don't want to remain there for very long. Our home is with others.[1]

Whether we prefer the tranquil village or the teeming metropolis, we wish to be with our kind. And to live together we must agree to certain ethical principles, at least at some minimal level.

[1] In his book *The Sane Society* (1955), Greenwich, CT: Fawcett Publications, and in other writings as well, Erich Fromm makes a strong case that humankind is both a part of nature yet also removed from it. We are still part animal but we are partly divine, too. As human beings we are no longer at home in the wilderness, our place is with others, and we must learn to live together.

These shared ethical principles are important for several reasons. They enable us to predict the behavior of others and form habits ourselves. Most importantly in our present context, the *polis* provides a set of rules that guide appropriate action for those who have not yet developed virtuous ways. For those without the benefit of self-discipline and "right desire" the *polis* structures social behavior. Yet, as Aristotle points out, the individual is primary. The *polis* exists of, and by, and for the individual. The purpose of the *polis* is the fulfillment of the individuals who comprise it.[2]

If this is true, if the purpose of the *polis* is to contribute to the growth of its members, we are in a position to judge the success or failure of a community. You may remember the distinction between real and apparent goods that we discussed in Chapter 5. Real goods fulfill human needs. Apparent goods give us pleasure but leave us unchanged and contribute nothing to the actualization of potentials. Food, shelter, friends, health, and liberty are real goods. Aristotle identifies goods of the body (such as health), goods of the soul (such as virtue, knowledge, and music) and external goods (money, a house, and "domestic tranquillity"). Diamonds, expensive cars, and good wine are pleasurable but do not make us better persons; they are apparent goods. There is nothing wrong with apparent goods or the pleasure they bring, as long as we understand their temporary impact on us.

A community in the form of a neighborhood, state, or nation can help us to acquire real goods or can make them difficult to obtain. While there are real goods that we must earn as individuals, the *polis* is responsible for providing some also. Justice, equality, and "the blessings of liberty" are only indirectly in the hands of individuals. These are provided by the *polis*. To the extent that a *polis* values real over apparent goods and promotes the general welfare, it encourages and assists individuals in their pursuit of happiness. But, to the

[2] See Verbeke, G. (1990). *Moral education in Aristotle.* Washington, D.C.: The Catholic University of America Press, Chapter 2, especially p. 77.

degree that a *polis* values apparent goods that yield only temporary pleasures, and devalues the real goods that matter, it fails its citizens. In this regard, Mortimer Adler[3] refers to the Preamble to the Constitution of the United States. It is the purpose of government, he says: "To establish justice, insure domestic tranquility, provide for the common defense, promote the general welfare, and secure the blessings of liberty."

The *polis* then can be our friend or it can work against us. Communities, neighborhoods, and tyrannical governments and regimes that emphasize inequality, injustice, material wealth, power, and greed deprive us of a decent human life. They deny us the possibility of happiness. In the final analysis it is actualization of human potential that makes a good human life. Communities in the form of families, villages, states, or nations that promote other, less noble goods, deprive us of what we need to live well. It is not only by creating restrictive and unfair policies that a *polis* can fail us. It can harm us by the very values it promotes.

Our time has often been criticized for its rampant materialism and commercialism and surely these criticisms are somewhat justified. However, economic well-being is important. Maslow's hierarchy of needs tells us that physiological, safety, and security motives are pre-potent and take precedence over the higher-order motives such as self-esteem and actualization. But once we have acquired enough material goods to satisfy our human needs, we would be well served to move on to the higher motives. Material goods are necessary to a point, in a certain amount, and to the degree that they fulfill our human needs. But beyond the *golden mean*, beyond the amount that is needed or required, the continued pursuit of material goods can be harmful.[4] Money, clothes, and a reliable car are good to a point,

[3] Adler, M. (1996/1970). *The time of our lives: The ethics of common sense.* New York: Fordham University Press.

[4] Lane, R. E. (2000). *The loss of happiness in market democracies.* New Haven, CT: Yale University Press.

but after that they become apparent goods, guiding us away from the things we need. The *polis* can promote either option, excess or prudent moderation leading to actualization.

IS ACTUALIZATION SELFISH?

We humans become members of a *polis* because it is our nature to do so. We share with others certain values, beliefs, and ethical principles that enable satisfying social relationships. Yet, at the same time, we seek fulfillment of our common and our uniquely individual potentials. Such pursuit may require that we perform certain acts that benefit the self. We need real goods and they may not be easy to come by. Even the best *polis* cannot provide all that we need to live well, nor should it. We have to *pursue* our happiness, just as Jefferson proclaimed.

Is our pursuit of real goods actually selfish, self-serving, and detrimental to others? How can we be good citizens of the *polis* and at the same time good to ourselves? Probably the most frequent criticism of Aristotle's actualization theory and all of its modern variations is that it leads to selfishness and self-indulgence. Critics proclaim, sometimes loudly and forcefully, that Aristotle's humanistic view not only promotes selfishness but overlooks our duty to others. They cite religious or philosophical principles that urge us to "love thy neighbor" and to place the interests of others above those of the self.

Erik Fromm[5] suggests that the origin of such criticism can be found in the religious writings of the Protestant Reformation where self-concern and self-love were viewed as wicked and shameful. Duty to God should come first. A little later, philosopher Emanuel

[5] Fromm, E. (1947). *Man for himself: An inquiry into the psychology of ethics.* Greenwich, CT: Fawcett Publications. See especially Chapter IV on "Problems of Humanistic Ethics."

Kant emphasized duty to others as well as to God. Fromm observes that the idea of selfishness as an evil is not restricted to religion and philosophy but became a cultural value "promulgated in home, school, motion pictures, books; indeed in all instruments of social suggestion as well. 'Don't be selfish' is a sentence which has been impressed upon millions of children, generation after generation."

But Fromm strongly rejects this view. Self-interest is not the same as selfishness. Self-interest is not contradictory to love for others. "If it is a virtue to love my neighbor as a human being, it must be a virtue – and not a vice – to love myself since I am a human being too." Love, concern, and respect for the self is not in opposition to love and respect for others. Fromm says that the truly selfish person does not really love himself but rather is incapable of any kind of love. Such a person may be self-protective, but not self-loving. Such a person cannot love himself and cannot love another either. Love, concern, and respect require strength and confidence and truly selfish people lack these. Their only concern is with protecting the flawed self that they must live with.

Love of the self is then not a bad thing, it's a good thing. We cannot respect others if we don't respect our selves. To the degree that we know our human needs and our unique potentials, and to the degree that we can fulfill them, we are better at loving others.

The effects of fulfillment extend far beyond the self. Aristotle's virtues include many socially productive actions. The virtuous person is able to and wants to act *justly*, treating others with equality and fairness. The virtuous person knows how to give to others. The virtue of *liberality* is the ability to correctly give of the self, not too little and not too much. *Friendship* was a major virtue for Aristotle and he discussed it at length. The virtuous person is *truthful* and *tactful* and has a good *sense of humor*. These are all virtues recognized by Aristotle and all contribute to the *polis* and to the well-being of others.

In this regard, Waterman,[6] in his discussion of *ethical individualism*, identifies three principles that characterize the actualized person. The first is freedom of choice that he calls *liberty*. The ethical individual allows others the *liberty* and opportunity to seek fulfillment and recognizes the right of all to pursue a good life. Second, Waterman cites the importance of respecting the *dignity* of others. The actualizing person sees others "as possessing a dignity comparable to ones own." And finally Waterman cites the importance of *justice and equity*, where all persons are permitted access to the goods needed for a good human life. Reviewing the results of many studies over the course of many years, Waterman concludes that fulfillment, or as he calls it *individualism*, is perfectly consistent with the "human good" – good for both the individual and the *polis*.

Clearly then, the fulfillment model of happiness does not, in any way, advocate selfishness. Fulfilled people are socially conscious and civic minded. Fulfillment of the self benefits the entire *polis*. Virtue contributes only good things, both to the self and to world. "Selfish" is not an appropriate description of the actualized individual.

There is another criticism of the actualization model that should be addressed. Some observe that the fulfillment theory accepts the expression of all potentials, even destructive ones. So if Joe Smith has the potential for violent, antisocial behavior, he must be allowed to express that possibility. Freud, of course, recognized that *thanatos*, the drive for death and destruction, was a powerful force in human beings. The need to destroy and injure is as human as the need for friendship and love. This argument against Aristotle's theory is more troublesome than the criticism regarding selfishness. Aristotle himself does not answer the charge but later thinkers have offered two principle counter arguments.

6 Waterman, A. S. (1984). *The psychology of individualism*. New York: Praeger Press.

Carl Rogers[7] believes that destructive, antisocial behavior stems not from any inherent potential within the person but rather from the world, which frustrates the expression of positive and constructive potentials. The frustration of natural inclinations can lead to atypical actions like aggression and destruction. That is, the world, through its obstructive powers, and not the person, is the source of the evil we too often witness.

Psychologists Michael and Lise Wallach[8] point out that humanistic psychologists like Maslow and Rogers, who followed Rousseau's philosophy that man is inherently good, have created a generation of selfish Americans. The humanistic view, they maintain, places entirely too much emphasis on the need for individual fulfillment and gives too little attention to the welfare of others. They refer to this view as the *minimalist approach* to ethics and roundly criticize its destructive consequences.

They also reject what they call the *authoritarian approach* to ethics suggesting that Western religion has so emphasized our inherent sinfulness that religion and other sources of external control are necessary. The Wallachs reject both the *authoritarian* and the *minimalist* positions on ethics. They believe that we humans possess some inherent potentials, including positive predispositions such as the desire to care for others, and praise the "good in our genes." But they also add that we cannot count on "spontaneous goodness" alone. Our potentials must be guided by the *polis*. We should "recognize that we can accept guidance, reminders, discipline, regulations, on behalf of others without giving up our freedom."

Rollo May[9] has offered still a different view. He suggests that both constructive and destructive potentials are found in all of us but it

[7] Rogers, C. S. (1961). *On becoming a person: A therapist's view of psychotherapy.* Boston: Houghton Mifflin.

[8] Wallach, M., & Wallach, L. (1983). *Psychology's sanction of selfishness.* San Francisco: W. H. Freeman & Co. See especially p. 90.

[9] May, R. (1969/1981). *Love and will.* New York: Dell, see p. 102.

is ultimately the mixture of the two that determines our actions. Taking a Freudian position where sex (love) and aggression (death) are ever present and opposing forces in our lives, he suggests that "in all stages of human development the experiences of love and death are interwoven." Actually, Freud's concept of sublimation suggested much the same idea. For Freud, the aggressive drives can be expressed in socially acceptable ways that are culture building rather than destructive. Thus, the soldier and the football player are engaged in constructive behaviors that allow them to express forces that might otherwise lead to antisocial behavior. Sublimation was an important idea in Freudian psychology. It suggests that our potentials and needs mix, combine, and synthesize to form emergent qualities. The bad in us can combine with the good to create, to produce, to achieve, and to fulfill.

In summary, our communities play an important role in the development and continuation of virtue. The *polis* can promote values that assist in fulfilling our potentials or it can stifle growth with harmful ideals and principles. Nations, cities, and even neighborhoods impact the happiness of their residents by the rules they create and the ideals they promote. The development of virtue requires not only "good upbringing" but a good *polis* as well.

Some claim that the goal of actualization is contrary to the welfare of the community. Religious, philosophical, and cultural voices have, from time to time, spoken strongly against the individualism promoted by the fulfillment model of well-being. However, a real understanding of actualization, the data from numerous studies, and countless instances of everyday experience refute that argument. The virtuous person is anything but selfish. Aristotle and his followers place the virtues of justice, equality, and the dignity of others in the forefront. Indeed, it is quite the opposite of what critics have claimed. Actualization of individual potentials contributes greatly to the *polis*.

Another criticism of the fulfillment model holds that even destructive potentials are encouraged. Because potentials probably do not manifest themselves in pure form but rather as composites, such a claim is probably a red herring. As Freud suggested long ago, sex and aggressive motives can, when combined with reason, become culture building rather than destructive. Aristotle's concept of virtue proclaimed the same idea much earlier. Desire, emotion, and action must be joined with and guided by reason. It is the composite, the mixture, the blend and synthesis that really counts. A raw, untouched, and unguided potential is probably as "mythical as the Jack of Spades." Potentials, like everything else, come synthesized and combined with other ingredients. They, like virtue, cannot be reduced to individual elements. Thus, the critics who claim that fulfillment theory promotes undesirable behavior must be questioned. Actualization is not selfish and it does not promote antisocial behavior. These presumed deficiencies of Aristotle's formula fail to weaken either its veracity or its enormous potential for promoting goodness.

17

Contemplation: A Different Kind of Happiness

> Contemplation of ultimate values becomes the same as contemplation of the nature of the world. Seeking truth ... may be the same as seeking beauty, order, oneness, perfection, rightness … Does science then become indistinguishable from art? religion? philosophy?
>
> Abraham Maslow, *The Farther Reaches of Human Nature* (1982)

The final chapters of Aristotle's *Nichomachaen Ethics* take a surprising turn. Throughout the *Ethics* we learn that a good human life requires intellectual and moral virtue. The key to happiness is found in virtue because courage, temperance, justice, friendship, and the like, allow us to acquire the real goods we need to fulfill potentials. A life of pleasure may be enjoyable in the short term but *practical wisdom* and the *golden mean* win out in the end. Virtue is good for the individual and good for the *polis*.

At the end of the *Ethics*, Aristotle seems to tell a different story: True happiness, he claims, is found in *contemplation*. Reason is the foundation of virtue, which enables us to navigate the everyday world. But reason can *also* lead us to another realm. It is possible to transcend the world of needs, material goods, and practical problems and enter the world of *forms* – the world of knowledge, truth, perfection,

---

Epigraph from Maslow, Abraham *The farther reaches of human nature* (1982) New York: Penguin Books p. 320. Permission granted by Ann Kaplan by personal communication.

and God. *Contemplation* is the means by which we can travel to the "ultimate concerns." Now, Aristotle returns us to his mentor, to Plato.

For Plato there is *matter* and there is *form*, stuff and "spirit." Plato urged us to leave the shadows of the cave (stuff) and embrace the world of eternal truths, the divine. Virtue may enable a good human life, which is what most of us want, but there are some who go further, transcending practical issues and moving closer to God. For Aristotle there is a caveat, however. We cannot overlook the physical world and focus exclusively on the eternal; the "real world" must be acknowledged. But for those who thrive in the everyday world there is the possibility of another kind of happiness.

TRANSCENDENCE

The idea that happiness lies in a transcendent world is nothing new. Early Christianity also embraced Plato's *forms*. In the early Middle Ages St. Augustine elevated the eternal while devaluing the material. The spiritual world, he claimed, revealed God's perfection but matter was ignoble and base, distracting us from the sacred. Aristotle, the founder of Western Science, would have disagreed: Humans are part of the *natural* world and cannot escape it. We must live in the physical as well as the spiritual realm.

In more modern times we find the shift from *matter* to *form*, from the earthly to the eternal, in many corners of psychology. William James, the founder of American psychology, left the discipline after writing "the most literate, the most provocative, and at the same time the most intelligible book on psychology that has ever appeared in English or in any other language"[1] to pursue his interests in philosophy and write the classic, *The Varieties of Religious Experience.*[2]

1 MacLeod, R. B. (Ed.) (1969). *William James: Unfinished business.* Washington D.C.: American Psychological Association, p. iii.

2 James, W. (1964/1902). *The varieties of religious experience.* New York: Mentor Books.

Carl Jung, Freud's famous disciple, also acknowledged a transition from the practical to the transcendent. A very spiritual man in his later years, Jung suggested stages of development beyond puberty where Freud left them, and proposed that in middle age we should begin to move away from the practical, work-a-day world to an interest in spirituality, religion, and wisdom.

Abraham Maslow's motivational stages reflect the same thinking. His stage of actualization, with its emphasis on values and ideals, comes only after the satisfaction of more practical needs relating to physiology, safety, belongingness, and self-esteem. Maslow also proposed a phenomenon called "*peak experience*," which most people have sometime but actualizing people have quite frequently. *Peak experiences* are feelings of closeness to the divine and of harmony with the universe. Maslow and his followers built on the idea of *peak experience* and eventually developed *transpersonal psychology*.[3] This approach focuses on spiritual and transcendent states of consciousness and seems very consistent with Aristotle's view of *contemplation* and spirituality as a higher form of well-being.

Another parallel to Aristotle's *contemplation* may be found in Lawrence Kohlberg's revision of his moral development theory.[4] You may remember that Kohlberg first proposed that morality develops in six stages. These stages were discussed in some detail in Chapter 14. It is interesting to find that later in his life, Kohlberg speculated about a new stage of moral development. As he tried to answer the question of why we should be moral he was led to postulate Stage 7: *Religious Stage*. Although Kohlberg began by trying to keep morality and religion separate, he eventually felt the need to join them. In the seventh stage the person experiences a connectedness with humanity

[3] Maslow, A. H. (1982). *The farther reaches of human nature*. New York: Penguin Books.

[4] Kohlberg, L. (1981). *The philosophy of moral development: Moral stages and the idea of justice* (*Essays on moral development*, Volume I). New York: Harper and Row.

and with the universe that compels moral judgments and actions. At this high level of development morality has religious significance, although it need not be associated with any particular religion. In Kohlberg we again find Aristotle's vision that spiritualism may follow the more practical concerns and the exercise of moral virtue.

NEUROTHEOLOGY

Religion and spiritualism have recently entered psychology from still another direction. When it was a young discipline, struggling for a place among the sciences, psychology avoided religious issues for fear of slipping back into the realm of philosophy. But over the years, having achieved a more secure position in academia, it developed the courage to address broader and more significant problems. Now there is a new field called *neurotheology*, the study of the brain processes underlying religious and spiritual states of consciousness.

It is increasingly recognized that religion and spiritualism play an important, even dominant, role in the lives of millions of people all over the world. For many on the planet spiritual experience shapes day-to-day activity and consciousness. Spiritualism may take a form prescribed by the traditional religions but it can also occur in states of meditation and unconventional transcending activities.

The opening line of Aristotle's *Metaphysics* reads: "All men by nature desire to know." Recently Andrew Newberg and colleagues[5] put it a little differently. We humans, they say, have an innate, involuntary drive to "make sense of things through the cognitive analysis of reality." They call this drive the *cognitive imperative*. We are built to think, understand, and find meaning in our existence. Even early man asked questions about birth and death and man's place in the universe. Trying to "make sense of things," our forbearers developed myths and rituals that often transported them into unusual states of

[5] Newberg, A., D'Aquili, E., & Rause, V. (2001). *Why God won't go away*. New York: Ballantine Books, see pp. 60, 114–115, and 19.

consciousness. Myth and ritual were the early paths to what we now call spiritualism.

Newberg's brain studies show how certain repetitive behaviors, such as those found in rituals, result in decreased activity of the parietal lobes. This brain area serves to locate objects and the self in space. When that area's activity is reduced, the boundary between the self and the rest of the world softens. As the defined self becomes blurry, the person tends to feel herself becoming part of a larger whole. This experience can be described as transcending the here and now, and is experienced as spiritual and or religious. Ritual activity like chanting or sustained prayer or *contemplation* can affect the parietal lobes and produce this feeling.

Newberg and colleagues scanned the brains of Tibetan Buddhists and Franciscan nuns as they meditated or prayed. They found scientific evidence of spiritualism. The experience is accompanied by increased activity in certain brain centers and a reduction of activity in other centers. Spiritualism is then more than just a psychological experience. It has biological roots in what the authors call the "machinery of transcendence."

Science has always shown little patience with phenomena that cannot be seen or measured. But things may be changing. The same "softening of the self" and the connection to an infinite, coherent wholeness has been observed for centuries in countless religious practices. Now we find that the brain is built for this form of understanding. Few of us have known the full-blown spiritual experiences that Newberg calls *absolute unitary being*, but many of us have known it, from time to time, in more mild forms. Newberg states, "Transcendent states, as we've seen, exist along a continuum of progressively higher levels of unitary being that ultimately leads to the point at which unity becomes absolute." As we progress toward the absolute, he suggests, we have created different approaches to religion but the same mystical spirituality is the source of all the world's religions.

Having begun as scientists investigating whether spirituality is a by-product of neurological activity, Newberg and colleagues appear forever changed by their findings: "the mind's machinery of transcendence may in fact be a window through which we can glimpse the ultimate realness of something that is truly divine." Newberg, D'Aquili, and Rause conclude as follows:

> The neurobiological roots of spiritual transcendence show that Absolute Unitary Being is a plausible, even probable possibility. Of all the surprises our theory has to offer – that myths are driven by biological compulsion, that rituals are intuitively shaped to trigger unitary states, that mystics are, after all not necessarily crazy, and that all religions are branches of the same spiritual tree – the fact that this ultimate unitary state can be *rationally* supported intrigues us the most. The realness of Absolute Unitary Being is not conclusive proof that a higher God exists, but it makes a strong case that there is more to human existence than sheer material existence. Our minds are drawn by the intuition of this deeper reality, this utter sense of oneness, where suffering vanishes and all desires are at peace. As long as our brains are arranged the way they are, as long as our minds are capable of sensing the deeper reality, spirituality will come to shape the human experience, and God, however we define that majestic, mysterious concept, will not go away.

RELIGION/SPIRITUALITY AND HAPPINESS

Psychologist Robert Emmons has recently explored the question of how religion and spirituality contribute to happiness and well-being.[6] Emmons affirms the importance of religion and spirituality to Americans, and indeed to the world, by citing some interesting statistics. According to a 1989 Gallup pole 90 percent of Americans believe in God or a supreme being. Two-thirds of these say that

[6] Emmons, R. (1999). *The psychology of ultimate concerns.* New York: Guilford Press.

religion plays an important role in their lives and 71 percent of Americans believe in life after death. Although we find enormous differences in religious practice, from traditional and structured worship to individually chosen forms of meditation and contemplation, America is truly a nation of believers.

Emmons is convinced, and his arguments are very persuasive, that the reason spirituality is so widely accepted is its importance to personality. Let's explore this idea a little further.

Emmons is a teleologist like Aristotle. He believes we are goal seeking: Everything we think or do is motivated in some way by a goal. Goals can be conscious or unconscious but in either case they direct our thoughts and actions. Most of us *want* to be rich, happy, good looking, well-liked, smart, and famous. Such goals direct behavior. Our actions are not random or guided by external stimuli alone. Rather, we are always in pursuit, always goal seeking, always searching. For Emmons religion and spirituality are high on the list of sought-after goals.

> Searches imply that there is something to be found; those end states are goals. A spiritual search involves the attempt to identify what is sacred and worthy of being committed to. The sacred refers to God, or related names for God, such as divine power, Supreme Being, Ultimate Reality, or Ultimate Truth.

This spiritual search can be very important to our well-being and happiness. Aristotle said that "all men desire to know," that we have a natural need to understand. Religion and spirituality can help in that pursuit. Here's how.

According to Emmons we have a multitude of goals that are, ideally, ordered and organized in a meaningful way. This is where religion and spirituality come in to play. They help to integrate our wants and desires; our goals. The Buddhists and others who practice Eastern religions and contemplative traditions, try to enter into a harmony with the cosmos. Their goal is to be at one and at peace with the universe. Such an ideal can become paramount and provide order for all other pursuits. The goal of being a "good human being" or practicing the principle of "Do unto others as you would wish done to you" can serve to order and integrate all the lesser goals. Religion and spirituality can order a life. Aristotelian scholar Richard Kraut[7] had much the same idea. He says of Aristotle, "just as he thinks that such ends as wealth, honor, pleasure, and virtue can be arranged in a hierarchy, some of these ends being for the sake of others, so he thinks that the virtues themselves can be arranged hierarchically."

From order comes meaning. If the words of a sentence are incorrectly ordered it will make no sense. But if the same words are correctly placed, the sentence is meaningful. It is generally accepted among psychologists, both past and present, that meaningfulness comes from relationships, connectedness, and wholeness. Baumeister[8] has likened meaning to a spider web attached to an array of objects. The web connects everything, linking separate parts and creating a meaningful whole. Emmons suggests that the ideas attained through religion and spirituality can help in this way to organize the various parts of our self. He states "The objective of religion, of all religions, is that of transformation of the person from fragmentation to integration." Religion, he says "has the potential to forge unity and coherence out of chaos and fragmentation." Religion can provide a "unifying philosophy of life. … It is the comprehensiveness of religion, in contrast to other belief systems, that is believed to account for the ability of religious sentiment to forge an harmonious pattern out of a patchwork of discordant impulses and strivings."

Both Carl Jung and C. S. Lewis liken personality to a wheel. The wheel has a central hub with spokes connected to a surrounding rim.

7 Kraut, R. (1989). *Aristotle on the human good*. Princeton, NJ: Princeton University Press, p. 13. Also philosopher Mark Chekola refers to a "life plan" or hierarchy of desires that, when successful in guiding our lives, brings about happiness. Chekola, M. (2007). Happiness, rationality, autonomy and the good life. *Journal of Happiness Studies*, *8*, 51–78.

8 Baumeister, R. (1991). *The meanings of life*. New York: Guilford Press.

When the spokes are in balance the wheel roles smoothly but when the spokes are misaligned, the rim and tire get out of round and the wheel wobbles as it rolls. You may remember this happening to a bicycle tire with broken spokes. The hub can be conceived as a central, unifying principle which aligns all the parts of the personality, the spokes. Another metaphor for religion might be the roots of a tree that hold the trunk upright and keep it stable while nourishing its branches and leaves.

However one wishes to conceive of religion and spirituality, it appears that many psychologists as well as theologians find that it can be a powerful force in our lives. Of course, there are those whose religious practice can be characterized as shallow and lacking the internalization of organizing principles and they will be unable to experience anything like the integration described by Emmons. But we must also recognize those who live their spiritualism on a daily basis. They demonstrate the kind of transforming religion that Emmons has in mind.

We cannot, with certainty, know exactly what Aristotle had in mind when he offered *contemplation* as the means to true happiness. But there is a strong possibility that he was referring to what we now call religion and spiritualism. The word "divine" appears six times in Chapter 7 of Book 10. In addition, there are several phrases that link the happiness of *contemplation* to the gods. For example "the life of the mind is divine," "As far as possible, we should become immortal," "the happiness of the mind is separate," "the activity of a god, which surpasses all other in blessedness, will be an activity of contemplation," "The life of the gods is completely happy, the life of men only so far as it has some resemblance to the gods' activity." Phrases such as these seem to support a transcendent view of *contemplation*.[9]

[9] Kraut, R. (1989) *Aristotle on the human good*. Princeton, NJ: Princeton University Press. See especially pp. 73–74 and footnote 52 for Kraut's view of the meaning of contemplation. He believes that Aristotle's contemplation lies at the apex of the hierarchy of virtues and is devoted to an understanding of

While he is usually considered the founder of Western Science and Rationalism there appears to be another side of Aristotle. Most philosophers have taken *contemplation* to mean the activity of study and the rational search for "first principles" or truths of the universe. But the frequent use of the term "divine" and repeated references to the gods permits an alternative interpretation.

We have already reviewed the tendency among many thoughtful people, when the time is right, to transcend the purely physical. *Matter* matters but so does *form*. Stuff is good but so are the gods. Albert Einstein, one of the greatest minds the world has known, suggested that "science without religion is lame and religion without science is blind." Recall that William James, the founder of American Psychology, moved on to *Varieties of Religious Experience* after completing his tenure in scientific psychology and concluded that religion allows us "to experience union with *something* larger than ourselves and in that union find our greatest peace." Maslow created transpersonal psychology in his later life. Kohlberg added a seventh stage, the religious stage, to his theory of moral development.

"the unmoved mover," or God. Broadie, S. (1991). *Ethics with Aristotle*. New York: Oxford University Press. See pp. 400–419. Broadie observes that the *Ethics* has "unquestionably, a religious dimension," p. 208. She also notes of Aristotle, "His statement in the *Ethics* that the intellect and its objects are of a divine nature is literal in the sense of being wholly serious – not rhetorical hyperbole and not a heuristic metaphor of passing usefulness. But at the same time we should not consider the statement a piece of finished doctrine. It is more like an intuitive starting point for any theory of God or the intellect, and hence is open to a variety of metaphysical and epistemological interpretations. *The Ethics* does not depend on one or another technical theory of God or intellect, but only on the principle to which any such theory would conform: that God, intellect and the object of intellect, what ever they are and however related, are of the same nature. No more than this is needed for Aristotelian ethics" (pp. 400–401). Philosopher Jonathan Lear (1999). Aristotle: The desire to understand. New York: Cambridge University Press, notes that man is able to become more of what he is by transcending his own nature. That is, we have the capacity to surpass the ethical life, the life of virtue, and through contemplation enter the realm of the divine. See especially Lear's section on "Mind's place outside of nature," pp. 293–320.

Before Aristotle, Plato tried to tell us of the importance of *forms*, the world of universal truths beyond the physical. Although Aristotle devoted most of his attention to the world of *matter*, he may never have left his mentors side on the issue of a good human life. Clearly, a person may become too removed from the physical world – too spiritual, too other-worldly, too religious – and only poorly adapted to the tasks of everyday life. The moral virtues are still central to a good human life, but they may also be a means to transcendence and contemplation. Several of the best minds in psychology, as well as in philosophy and theology, agree: Spirituality may be the center of the target. Fulfillment may extend beyond the satisfaction of deprivation needs and beyond the actualization of potentials to the farther reaches of human consciousness. Religion and spirituality have been with us from the very beginning, and perhaps when they are grasped in their deepest, most meaningful, and profound form, they provide the ultimate form of happiness.

REFERENCES

Adler, M. (1996/1970). *The time of our lives: The ethics of common sense.* New York: Fordham University Press.

Altman, I. (1975). *The environment and social behavior: Privacy, personal space, territory, crowding.* Monterey, CA: Brooks/Cole Publishing Co.

Annas, J. (1993). *The morality of happiness.* New York: Oxford University Press.

Aristotle, *The Nicomachean ethics*, Ross, D. (1986). New York: Oxford University Press.

Politics: The philosophy of Aristotle. (1963). Trans. by A.E. Wardman & J.L. Creed, New York: Mentor Book, New American Library.

Politics. In R. M. Hutchins & M. J. Adler (Eds.), *Great books of the Western world.* (1952). Chicago: Encyclopedia Britannica.

Armstrong, K. (1993). *A history of God: The 4000 year quest of Judaism, Christianity and Islam.* New York: Ballantine Books.

Arrington, R. (1998). *Western ethics: An historical introduction.* Malden, MA: Blackwell Publishers Inc.

Augustine, S. The city of God. In R. M. Hutchens & M. J. Adler (Eds.), *Great Books of the Western World.* (1952). Book 19, Chapter 20. Chicago: Encyclopedia Britannica.

Bar-On, R. (2006). The Bar-On model of social and emotional intelligence (ESI)(1). *Psicothema, 18*, supl., 13–25. Can be found at http://www.eiconsortium.org/reprints/bar-on_model_of_emotional-social_intelligence.htm

(2001). Emotional intelligence and self-actualization. In J. Ciarrochi, J. Forgas, & J.D. Mayer (Eds.), *Emotional Intelligence in everyday life: A scientific inquiry.* New York: Psychology Press.

Bauer, J. J., McAdams, D. P., & Pals, J. (2008). Narrative identity and eudaimonic well-being. *Journal of Happiness Studies, 9*, 81–104.

Baumeister, R. (1991). *The meanings of life.* New York: Guilford Press.

(1987). How the self became a problem: A psychological review of historical research. *Journal of Personality and Social Psychology, 52*, 163–176.

(1986). *Identity: Cultural change and the struggle for self.* New York: Oxford University Press.

Bjork, D. W. (1983). *The compromised scientist: William James in the development of American psychology.* New York: Columbia University Press.

Brickman, P., Coats, D., & Janoff-Bulman, R. (1978). Lottery winners and accident victims: Is happiness relative? *Journal of Personality and Social Psychology, 36*, 917–927; Luter, M. Book Review: Winning a Lottery Brings No Happiness! (2007). *Journal of Happiness Studies, 8*, 155–160.

Broadie, S. (1991). *Ethics with Aristotle.* New York: Oxford University Press.

Carlyle, T. (1827). *Critical and miscellaneous essays.*

Carter, S. L. (1998). *Civility: Manners, morals, and the etiquette of democracy.* New York: Harper Collins.

Chekola, M. (2007). Happiness, rationality, autonomy and the good life. *Journal of Happiness Studies, 8*, 51–78.

Ciarrochi, J., Forgas, J., & Mayer, J. D. (Eds.) (2001). *Emotional intelligence in everyday life: A scientific inquiry.* Philadelphia, PA: Psychology Press.

Clausen, J. A. (1993). *American lives: Looking back at the children of the Great Depression.* New York: The Free Press.

Cohen, E. (2003). *What would Aristotle do?* Amherst, NY: Prometheus Books.

Csikszentmihalyi, M. (1993). *The evolving self: A psychology for the third millennium.* New York: HarperCollins Publishers.

(1990). *Flow: The psychology of optimal experience.* New York: Harper Perennial a division of Harper/Collins Publishers.

Csikszentmihalyi, M., Rathunde, K., Whalen, S., & Wong, M. (1993). *Talented teenagers: The roots of success and failure.* London. Cambridge University Press.

Damasio, A. (1994). *Descartes' error: Emotion, reason, and the human brain.* New York: Avon Press.

DeCharms, R. (1968). *Personal causation: The internal affective determinants of behavior.* New York: Academic Press.

Deci, E. (1980). *The psychology of self-determination.* Lexington, MA: Lexington Books.

(1975). *Intrinsic motivation.* New York: Plenum Press.

Deci, E. L., Koestner, R., & Ryan, R. M. (1999). A meta-analytic review of experiments examining the effects of extrinsic rewards on intrinsic motivation. *Psychological Bulletin.* 25, 627–668.

Deci, E. L., & Ryan, R. M. (1985). *Intrinsic motivation and self-determination in human behavior.* New York: Plenum Press.

Diener, E. (2000). Subjective well-being. *American Psychologist, 55*, 34–43.

Diener, E., Horwitz, J., & Emmons, R. (1985). "Happiness of the very wealthy." *Social Indicators, 16*, 263–274.

Einstein, A. (1978). *Ideas and opinions.* New York: Dell Publishing Co.

Elias, M. J., Hunter, L., & Kress, J. S. (2001). Emotional intelligence and education. In J.Ciarrochi, J. Forgas, & J. D. Mayer (Eds.), *Emotional intelligence in everyday life: A scientific inquiry.* New York: Psychology Press.

Elias, M., Tobias, S., & Freidlander, B. (1999). *Emotionally intelligent parenting. How to raise a self-disciplined, responsible, socially skilled child.* New York: Random House.

Ellis, A., & Harper R. A. (1961/1997). *A guide to rational living.* North Hollywood, CA: Wilshire Book Company.

Emmons, R. (1999). *The psychology of ultimate concerns.* New York: Guilford Press.

Epstein, S. (1998). *Constructive thinking: The key to emotional intelligence.* Westport, CT: Praeger.

Epstein, S., & Brodsky, A. (1993). *You're smarter than you think.* New York: Simon & Shuster.

Epstein, S., & Meier, P. (1989). Constructive thinking: A broad coping variable with specific components. *Journal of Personality and Social Psychology, 57*, 332–350.

Erikson, E. H. (1964). *Insight and responsibility* New York: W.W. Norton & Co. Inc.

Fortenbaugh, W. W. (2002/1975). *Aristotle on emotion.* London: Duckworth.

Fowers, B. J. (2005). *Virtue and psychology: Pursuing excellence in ordinary practices.* Washington, D.C.: American Psychological Association.

Franklin, S. (1994). *An examination of Aristotle's concept of virtue and its relationship to well-being.* Paper presented at the Meeting of the Western Psychological Association. Los Angeles, CA.

Franklin, S., & Torzynski, R. (1993). *Virtue and well-being: Evidence for Aristotle's eudaemonic theory of happiness.* Paper presented at the Meeting of the Western Psychological Association. Phoenix, AZ.

Freedman, J. (1978). *Happy people: What happiness is, who has it, and why.* New York: Harcourt Brace Jovanovish.

Freud, S. (1962/1930). *Civilization and its discontents.* New York: W.W. Norton & Co. Inc.

Frey, B. S., & Jegen, R. (1999). *Motivation crowding theory: A survey of empirical evidence.* Working Paper No. 26. Working Paper Series ISSN 1424–0459. Institute for Empirical Research in Economics, Universe of Zurich. Available at www.landecon.cam.ac.uk/speer/iewwp026.pdf

Fromm, E. (1955). *The sane society.* Greenwich, CT: Fawcett Publications, Inc.

(1947). *Man for himself: An inquiry into the psychology of ethics.* Greenwich, CT: Fawcett Publications.

Gardner, H. (1999). *The disciplined mind: What all students should understand.* New York: Simon & Schuster.

(1993). *Multiple intelligences: The theory in practice.* New York: Basic Books.

(1983). *Frames of mind: The theory of multiple intelligences.* New York: Basic Books.

Gilligan, C.(1982). *In a different voice: Psychological theory and women's development.* Cambridge: Harvard University Press.

Goleman, D. (1999). *Working with emotional intelligence.* New York: Bantam Books.

(1998). What makes a good leader. *Harvard Business Review,* Nov./Dec.

(1995). *Emotional intelligence.* New York: Bantam Books.

Gottman, J. (1997). *The heart of parenting: How to raise an emotionally intelligent child.* New York: Simon & Schuster.

Hagerty, M.R. (1999). Testing Maslow's hierarchy of needs: National quality-of-life across time. *Social Indicators Research, 46,* 249–271.

Hall, G.S. (1954/1961). *A primer of Freudian psychology.* New York: Mentor Books.

Hedlund, J., & Sternberg, R.J. (2000). Too many intelligences? Integrating social, emotional and practical intelligence. In R. Bar-On & J. D.Parker. *The handbook of emotional intelligence: Theory, development, assessment and application at home, school, and in the work place.* San Francisco: Jossey-Bass.

Huitt, W. (2004). *Moral and character development.* Educational Psychology Interactive. Valdosta, GA: Valdosta State University. Retrieved November 2, 2005, from http://Chiron.valdosta.edu/whuitt/col.morchr.html

James, W. (1969/1892). *Psychology: Briefer course.* London: Collier-Macmillan Ltd.

(1893). *Psychology: Briefer course.* New York: Henry Holt and Co.

Kashdan, T.B., Biswas-Diener, R., & King, L.A. (in press). Reconsidering happiness: The costs of distinguishing between hedoncis and eudaimonia. *Journal of Positive Psychology.*

Kasser, T., & Ryan, R.M. (1993). A dark side of the American Dream: Correlates of financial success as a central life aspiration. *Journal of Personality and Social Psychology, 65,* 410–422.

Kaufmann, W. (Ed.) (1961). *Existentialism: From Dostoevsky to Sartre.* Cleveland: Meridian Books.

King, L., & Napa, C. K. (1998). What makes a life good. *Journal of Personality and Social Psychology, 75*, 156–165.

Klinger, E. (1977). *Meaning and void: Inner experience and the incentives in people's lives.* Minneapolis: University of Minnesota Press.

Kohlberg, L. (1981). *The philosophy of moral development: Moral stages and the idea of justice (Essays on moral development,* Volume I). New York: Harper and Row.

(1976). Moral stages and moralization. In T. Lickona (Ed.), *Handbook of socialization theory.* New York: Holt, Rinehart & Winston.

Kraut, R. (1989). *Aristotle on the human good.* Princeton, NJ: Princeton University Press.

Kroger, J. (2004). *Identity in adolescence: The balance between self and other.* New York: Routledge, Taylor & Francis Group.

Lane, R. E. (2000). *The loss of happiness in market democracies.* New Haven, CT: Yale University Press.

Lazarus, R. S., & Lazarus, B. N. (1994). *Passion and reason: Making sense of our emotions.* New York: Oxford University Press.

(1991). *Emotion and adaptation.* New York: Oxford University Press.

Lear, J. (1999). *Aristotle: The desire to understand.* New York: Cambridge University Press.

LeDoux, J. (1996). *The emotional brain.* New York: Simon and Schuster.

Leyhausen, P. (1970). The communal organization of solitary mammals. In H. M. Proshansky, W. H. Ittelson, & L. G. Rivlin (Eds.), *Environmental psychology: Man and his physical setting.* New York: Holt, Rinehart and Winston,

Logue, A. W. (1995). *Self-control: Waiting until tomorrow for what you want today.* Englewood Cliffs, NJ: Prentice Hall.

MacLeod, R. B. (Ed.) (1969). *William James: Unfinished business.* Washington, D.C.: American Psychological Association.

May, R. (1969/1981). *Love and will.* New York: Dell.

Marcia, J. E. (1980). Identity in adolescence. In J. Adelson (Ed.), *Handbook of adolescent psychology.* New York: Wiley.

Maslow, A. (1970/1954). *Motivation and personality.* New York: Harper & Row Publishers.

(1982). *The farther reaches of human nature.* New York: Penguin Books.

Mearns, D., & Thorne, B. (2000). *Person-centered therapy today: New frontiers in theory and practice.* Thousand Oaks, CA: Sage Publications.

McKinnon, C. (1999). *Character, virtue theories, and the vices.* Ontario, Canada: Broadview Press.

McMahon, D. M. (2006). *Happiness: A history.* New York: Atlantic Monthly Press.

Mill, J. S. (1952/1861). *Utilitarianism.* In R. M. Hutchins & M. J. Adler (Eds.), the *Great Books of the Western World*, Chapter 2.

Milton, J. (2002). *The road to Malpsychia: Humanistic psychology and our discontents.* San Francisco: Encounter Books.

Moos, R.H., & Insel, P.M. (Eds.) (1974). *Issues in social ecology: Human milieus.* Palo Alto, CA: National Press Books.

Morris, D. (1967). *The naked ape: A zoologists' study of the human animal.* New York: McGraw-Hill Publishers.

(1969). *The human zoo.* New York: McGraw Hill Publishers.

Morris, T. (1997). *If Aristotle ran General Motors.* New York: Owl Book, Henry Holt and Co.

Moyers, B. (1981). PBS Six Great Ideas: Truth-Goodness-Beauty-Liberty-Equality-Justice. (The Television Series) with Mortimer Adler. From the Aspen Institute in Colorado.

Myers, D. G. (1992). *The pursuit of happiness: Discovering the pathways to well-being and enduring personal joy.* New York: Harper Collins Publishers.

Nettle, D. (2005). *Happiness: The science behind your smile.* New York: Oxford University Press.

Newberg, A., D'Aquili, E., & Rause, V. (2001). *Why God won't go away.* New York: Ballantine Books.

Noddings, N. (2003). *Happiness and education.* Cambridge, UK: Cambridge University Press.

Norton, D. L. (1976). *Personal destinies: A philosophy of ethical individualism.* Princeton, NJ: Princeton University Press.

Norzick, R. (1974). *Anarchy, state and utopia.* New York: Basic Books.

Oakley, J. (1992). *Morality and the emotions.* New York: Routledge.

O'Toole, J. (2005). *Creating the good life: Applying Aristotle's wisdom to find meaning and happiness.* New York: Rodale.

Park, N., & Peterson, C. (2006). Character strengths and happiness among young children: Content analysis of parental descriptions. *Journal of Happiness Studies, 7,* 323–341.

Peterson, C., & Seligman, M. E. P. (2004). *Character strengths and virtues: A handbook and classification.* Oxford: Oxford University Press.

Piaget, J. (1932/1965). *The moral judgment of the child.* New York: Basic Books.

Power, M., & Dalgleish, T. (1997). *Cognition and emotion: From order to disorder.* Hove, East Sussex, UK: Psychology Press.

Rogers, C. (1961). *On becoming a person: A therapist's view of psychotherapy.* Boston: Houghton Mifflin.

Ross, E.D. (1997). Cortical representation of emotions. In M. Timble. & J. Cummings(Eds.), *Behavioural neurology.* Oxford: Butterworth-Heinemann.

Ryan, R.M., Huta, V., & Deci, E.L. (2008). Living well: A self-determination theory perspective of eudaimonia. *Journal of Happiness Studies, 9*, 139–170.

Ryan, R. M., & Deci, E. L. (2000). Self-determination theory and the facilitation of intrinsic motivation, social development, and well-being. *American Psychologist, 55*, 68–78.

Ryff, C.D., (1989). Happiness is everything or is it? Explorations on the meaning of psychological well-being. *Journal of Personality and Social Psychology, 57*, 1069–1081.

Ryff, C. D., & Singer, B. (2007). Know thyself and become what you are: A eudaimonic approach to psychological well-being. *Journal of Happiness Studies, 9*, 13–39.

Ryff, C. D., & Singer, B. H. (2002). Flourishing under fire: Resilience as a prototype of challenged thriving. In C. L. M. Keys & J. Haidt (Eds.), *Flourishing: Positive psychology and the life well-lived.* Washington, D.C.: American Psychological Association.

(1998). The contours of positive human health. *Psychological Inquiry, 9*, 1–28.

Salovey, P., & Mayer, J.D. (1990). Emotional intelligence. *Imagination, Cognition, and Personality, 9*, 185–211.

Seligman, M. E. P. (2002). *Authentic happiness.* New York: Free Press.

(1975). *Helplessness.* San Francisco: W. H. Freeman and Co.

(1971). Phobias and preparedness. *Behavior Therapy, 2*, 307–320.

Sherman, N. (1999). *Aristotle's ethics: Critical essays.* Lanham, MD: Rowman & Littlefield Publishers

(1997). *Making a necessity of virtue.* New York: Cambridge University Press.

Skinner, B.F. (1948). *Walden two.* New York: The Macmillan Co.

Snyder, C.R., & Lopez, S.J. (Eds.) (2002). *Handbook of positive psychology.* New York: Oxford University Press.

Sternberg, R.J. (2001).Measuring the intelligence of an Idea: How intelligent is the idea of emotional intelligence? In J. Ciarrochi, J. P. Forgas, & J. D. Mayer. *Emotional intelligence in everyday life: A scientific inquiry.* New York: Psychological Press.

Tannsjo, T. Narrow Hedonism. (2007). *Journal of Happiness Studies, 8*, 79–98.

Torzynski, R. (1994). *Well-being and virtue: Investigating Aristotle's theory of eudaimonia.* Masters Thesis. Department of Psychology, California State University Fresno. Fresno, CA.

Vallerand, R.J., Blanchard, C., Mageau, G.A., Leonard, C.R., Koestner, R., & Gagne, M., (2003). Les Passions de l'Ame: On obsessive and harmonious passion. *Journal of Personality and Social Psychology, 85*, 756–767.

Vanier, J.(2001). *A guide to a good life: Happiness, Aristotle for the new century.* New York: Arcade Publishing.

Veatch, H.B. (1962). *Rational man: A modern interpretation of Aristotle's ethics.* Indiana: University of Indiana Press.

Verbeke, G. (1990). *Moral education in Aristotle.* Washington, D.C.: The Catholic University of America Press.

Wallach, M., & Wallach, L. (1983). *Psychology's sanction of selfishness.* San Francisco: W.H. Freeman & Co.

Walen, S.R., DiGiuseppe, R., & Wessler, R.L. (1980). *A practitioner's guide to rational emotive therapy.* New York: Oxford University Press.

Waterman, A.S., Schwartz, S.J., & Conti, R. (2008). The implications of two conceptions of happiness (hedonic enjoyment and eudaimonia) for the understanding of intrinsic motivation. *Journal of Happiness Studies, 9*, 41–79.

Waterman, A.S. (Ed.) (1985). *Identity in adolescence: Processes and contents.* New Directions for Child Development. #30, Dec.1985. San Francisco: Jossey-Bass Inc.

(1984). *The psychology of individualism.* New York: Praeger Press.

Watson, J.B. (1970/1924). *Behaviorism.* New York: W.W. Norton & Co. Inc.

Wethington, E. (2003). Turning points as opportunities for psychological growth. In C.L.M. Keys & J. Haidt (Eds.), *Flourishing: Positive psychology and the life well-lived.* Washington, D.C.: American Psychological Association.

White, R. (1959). Motivation reconsidered: The concept of competence. *Psychological Review, 66*, 297–333.

Wicker, F.W., Brown, G., Wiehe, J.A., Hagen, A.S., & Reed, J.L. (1993). On reconsidering Maslow: An examination of the deprivation/domination proposition. *Journal of Research in Personality, 27*, 118–133.

INDEX